# Butterflies

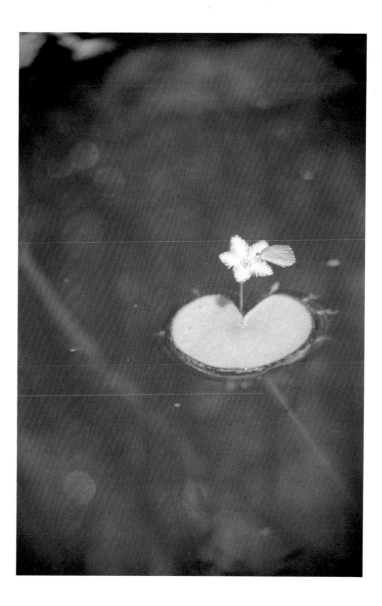

1. *left:* Pieridae: *Phoebis sp.,* United States. Feeding on hibiscus in a Florida garden.

2. *above:* An Australian Pierid finds safety in an isolated setting into which its color blends.

*Overleaf:*
3. Heliconiidae. Possibly *Heliconius sara.*

4. *left inset:* Nymphalidae: *Phyciodes tharos.* This little butterfly is found throughout the eastern United States from late April until midsummer. It can be seen in open meadows, especially where the aster—the plant on which its eggs are laid—grows. In the warmer parts of its range, it may have as many as five broods.

5. *right inset:* Nymphalidae: *Parthenos sylvia,* New Guinea. A large but not showy butterfly, with a rather uncommon kind of geometric markings.

6. *left:* Ithomiidae: clearwing butterfly from Peru.

7. *Inset left:* Ithomiidae: clearwing butterflies from Costa Rica.

8. *above:* Ithomiidae: clearwing butterflies from Costa Rica. The species of this family, shown here and in plates 6 and 7, resemble each other so closely that it is nearly impossible to tell them apart, on the wing. The Pierid, *Dismorphia fortunata* (plate 11), derives protection by closely resembling the poisonous Ithomiidae.

*Overleaf:*
9. Heliconiidae: *Heliconius sp.* (probably *Heliconius sara*), Trinidad.

HARRY N. ABRAMS, INC., *Publishers*, NEW YORK

# Butterflies

PHOTOGRAPHS BY KJELL B. SANDVED

TEXT BY JO BREWER

10. Papilionidae: *Parnassius clodius,* United States. In the *Parnassius* butterfly the antennae are always short. All the Parnassians inhabit high mountain ranges, with altitudes of 6,000 feet and over. In all species, the male, while mating, leaves a hard case on the abdomen on the female, preventing her from mating again.

Library of Congress Cataloging in Publication Data
Brewer, Jo.
  Butterflies.
  1. Butterflies.   I. Sandved, Kjell Bloch,
1922-     ill. II. Title.
QL544.B73      595.7'89      74-23357
ISBN 0-8109-2064-6

Library of Congress Catalogue Card Number: 74-23357
Published by Harry N. Abrams, Incorporated, New York, 1978

Acknowledgment is made with thanks to Little, Brown and Company for
permission to quote "Sing Cocoon" by David McCord (which
originally appeared in *The New Yorker*), from his volume *Odds Without
Ends* ( © David McCord 1949); and "The Lepidopterist" by
Ogden Nash, from his volume *The Private Dining Room and Other Verses*
( © Ogden Nash 1952).

# CONTENTS

11. Pieridae: *Dismorphia fortunata.*
A clearwing butterfly from Costa
Rica.

# FOREWORD

A yellow cloud of butterflies rose from the bank of the great river as I passed by
and quietly settled again behind me. Nearby were gigantic kapok, or silk-cotton,
trees (*Ceiba pentandra*). The trunks were 9 feet in diameter, forming large, board-
like buttresses. Arm-thick lianas hung down from their branches, high, high up
in the air, something I had never seen before. This was my introduction to the
Amazon. I was standing in the delta area near Belém.

Inside the dense forest the deep silence is only occasionally broken by the
distant roar of howler monkeys. Though butterflies, especially Pierids, are numerous in open areas, in the dense Amazonian climax forest, untouched by man,
they are sparse. An occasional furtive Satyrid, the wood nymph, flitters near the
ground in the black shade of the towering trees. It is only when one of these
giant trees falls to the ground and a flowery vegetation and secondary forest
eventually take over that the butterflies and moths congregate here.

The whole scene is made more awesome when we remember how deeply it
had impressed Darwin a century and a half earlier:

> The day has passed delightfully. Delight itself, however, is a weak term to express
> the feelings of a naturalist who, for the first time, has wandered by himself in a

Brazilian forest. The elegance of the grasses, the novelty of the parasitical plants, the beauty of the flowers, the glossy green of the foliage, but above all the general luxuriance of the vegetation, filled me with admiration. . . . To a person fond of natural history, such a day as this brings with it a deeper pleasure than he can ever hope to experience again. (Charles Darwin, *The Voyage of the Beagle*.)

In this wonderful natural laboratory of the Brazilian wilderness a man could spend his whole life attempting to learn the interrelationships and behavior of the butterflies and moths inhabiting only a few square miles and still leave a wealth of fascinating material unexplored. For instance, the life histories and larval stages of only a small percentage of the hundreds of species in this area are known. So many interesting and important data remain to be learned and await the future student.

My next expedition to the Amazon area brought me to the upper region of Peru, near the village of Tingo Maria. Here the butterflies are for the most part different from those in the Belém area. This journey took my helper and me down the eastern slopes of the Andes from the snow-clad mountains through gorgeous valleys and steep chasms. A slippery path among huge boulders led us to a cool spring under an overhanging rock. In this little spot we got photos of three different species of butterflies, a welcome bath, and delicious drinking water.

I shall never forget the exhilarating pleasure of going out early in the beautiful tropical morning the following day into a little valley next to the village. The tiny, inch-deep trickling stream there is a tributary to a tributary to a tributary to the mighty Amazon. I settled down among some flowering bushes and at 8:30 A.M., triggered by their internal biological clock, the butterflies started arriving.

I was amazed to see the many species of butterflies drinking there. They were very skittish during our moments of confrontation, but after hours of crawling slowly among them, I managed to get some of my best "wet-belly" close-up photographs of the Nymphalid butterfly *Callicore sp.* and the difficult-to-photograph Riodinid and several Lycaenid butterflies. Seeing the drinking butterflies highly magnified through my camera's close-up lens was like discovering a new realm of the natural ground-level world. The image I saw was a giant, sparkling rainbow-colored butterfly between boulders in a roaring stream that threatened to wash it away any minute. It drank and drank and was squirting out a droplet from the tip of its abdomen every five seconds. As I lay watching, my mind wandered into a daydream: the sparkling droplets were rendered into human tears of sympathy for the threatened survival of the poor little creature, which can neither hear nor utter any sound, in the wake of man's reduction of its habitats.

The cramp in my neck muscles brought me back to reality. When should I shoot? Is this the best shot I can get? Will they fly away? I am faced with infinite choices. The scene will never be repeated exactly the same way. All I can capture of my wonderful discovery is one tiny segment, one little frame of the ever-changing scenes in my viewfinder. And many a time I have waited too long; a cloud hides the sun, it starts to rain, or the butterfly suddenly takes off.

On a recent trip to the Cameron Highlands in Malaysia, I was fortunate to find the most regal butterfly of them all: the ornithoptera, or bird-wing butterfly, *Trogonoptera brookiana*. I was traveling with a Malaysian helper of Chinese extraction, Choo See Yan, when we came upon a little stream flowing down a narrow valley. After half a day of walking and stumbling among slippery boulders, we came to a small settlement. Farther up we came to the place Choo See Yan knew was frequented by the ornithoptera. There they were—several perfect large specimens drinking on the wet sand.

Darwin's friend and "nearly co-author" of *The Origin of Species*, the English naturalist Alfred Russel Wallace, describes in his classic book *The Malay Archipelago* his impression on seeing this butterfly for the first time:

> I found it to be as I had expected, a perfectly new and most magnificent species, and one of the most gorgeously coloured butterflies in the world. Fine specimens of the male are more than seven inches across the wings, which are velvety black and fiery orange. . . . The beauty and brilliancy of this insect are indescribable, and none but a naturalist can understand the intense excitement I experienced when I at length captured it. On taking it out of my net and opening the glorious wings, my heart began to beat violently, the blood rushed to my head, and I felt much more like fainting than I have done when in apprehension of immediate death. I

had a headache the rest of the day, so great was the excitement produced by what
will appear to most people a very inadequate cause.

I too felt a violent heartbeat when I saw and was able to photograph this insect,
but fortunately I did not get the headache.

On the way back, however, we had to pass close by one of the houses in the
settlement and were greeted by a most unfriendly dog. Before I knew what was
happening, the dog bit my hand to the bone and hung on to it, shaking it and
growling fiercely. We finally managed to drive the creature off, and with the
Malaysians in full pursuit he disappeared into the jungle. Making circling mo-
tions at their heads, the Malaysians indicated that the dog was mad. I went
down to the stream to clean my wound, which was all I could do, since we were
not prepared for such an emergency and there were no medical facilities in the
area. I was wondering all the while if rabies was worse than schistosomiasis. Ob-
taining pictures of rare species in exotic places is not without its risks. We returned to our camp to await the worst. Two days later, since I was fine, we went
back to the same valley and resumed our search. Passing the village again we
crossed the river first, but fortunately the dog was nowhere to be seen.

My photographic equipment normally consists of three or four Nikon cameras.
My standard close-up lens is the Micro-Nikkor PC Auto, 1:3.5, 55mm, perma-
nently fitted out with an oversized 62mm filter holder, which can then be used
on most of my other lenses.

For extreme close-ups, however, Zeiss Luminar lenses are considerably
sharper. The Luminar lenses come in five focal lengths: 100mm, 63mm, 40mm,
25mm, and 16mm; the one I have used most frequently is the 40mm, which has

12. Nymphalidae: *Cethosia
chrysippe,* New Guinea. This is
considered by many to be the mo
beautiful butterfly in the Australi
region. It is orange and dark
brown, but when the sun shines
it—especially on a newly emerg
butterfly—it takes on a psychede
pink and purple glow that is
breathtaking.

16

its maximum performance at 5:1 magnification, or for specimens from 5mm to 10mm long. These lenses do not have an automatic diaphragm, so I have devised a semi-automatic diaphragm for them. This system works very well with tiny insects in the field. Also, when photographing scale formations in the wings of butterflies and moths in the laboratory, I use these Zeiss Luminar lenses with bellows up to a yard long. The Luminar lenses were used for nearly all the close-ups of butterfly wings and details of scale design shown here. For wide-angle lenses, I find I more frequently use the 24mm, 1:2.8, rather than the 28mm or the 20mm.

Until the Vivitar Series 1, 1:3.5, Macro-Focusing Auto Zoom 70—210mm appeared on the market, I had to make use of a short mount 135mm on bellows with all the exposure problems this system has. The Vivitar lens is a joy for photographing butterflies. One can even learn to push-focus the lens while holding the camera with one hand.

My movies of butterfly behavior were all taken with the 16mm Beaulieu camera. My special "butterfly lenses" were two Macro-Kilar lenses: the 40mm, which I fitted out with a semi-automatic diaphragm, and the excellent 90mm. For butterflies in the canopies of high tropical trees I have used the Century Tele-Athenar 300mm.

On occasion I have been able to photograph butterflies in the rain; my field helper holds the electronic strobe light, and I sneak up slowly to a butterfly resting on the underside of a leaf. Electronic strobe lights always malfunction in the tropics when the humidity approaches 100 percent. This was for years one of my worst problems in dark areas of the jungle. In recent years I have managed to condition my strobes so that they now work under the wettest of circumstances. Natural sunlight gives a more pleasing effect for photographing in nature, but for many of my extreme close-ups an electronic strobe light with an exposure of 1/2000 of a second is needed; this speed stops any motion and gives the maximum depth of focus.

Butterflies—caterpillars in wedding gowns—are certainly among nature's most beautiful gifts. They were well established on this planet millions of years before man and are found in all latitudes between 50° south and 70° north.

There are two areas in the world, however, where the greatest speciation, differences of habitats, and diversity occur. One region is on the eastern slopes of the Andes—the upper Amazon, bordering on Peru, Colombia, and Venezuela. The other area, just as rich but different, is the region arching from New Guinea, Indonesia, and Malaya up to Bhutan. On photographic safaris to these areas I have taken thousands of shots of butterflies and other insects.

Though there are many areas where butterflies still exist in abundance, they are slowly, inexorably being crowded out of existence. In Sikkim, the "Butterfly Paradise" on the slopes of the Himalayas, many species are becoming extinct. Deforestation, soil erosion, and malaria-control programs with DDT have been followed by a decline in numbers of species.

"The butterflies—what an educated sense of beauty they have," wrote Phil Robinson in his delightful little book *The Poets and Nature* (London, 1893). "They seem only an ornament to society, and yet, if they were gone, how substantial would be their loss!"

Forty years later, in 1932, Dr. Austin H. Clark stated in the Smithsonian publication "The Butterflies of the District of Columbia":

> There has been very considerable change in the faunal balance since I became a resident of the District of Columbia twenty-four years ago. These changes have been evident to everyone with even a casual interest in butterflies. Several species have not been seen in the District for many years, while others have disappeared quite recently. Many that presumably were once common are now very rare or merely casual. Several others occur only in isolated colonies in very limited areas of boggy ground which are certain to be filled in within the next few years, resulting in the elimination of all traces of the butterflies.

I personally have noticed a similar gradual decline in the species of butterflies since I became a resident of the District of Columbia fifteen years ago. It is often the more attractive species with highly specific food plants which are crowded out and seem less able to survive than the sparrow of the Lepidoptera, the cabbage butterfly.

But today Dr. Howard Evans writes in his book *Life on a Little-known Planet*:

These items [the declining of butterflies] struck home to me, as not long ago I visited some of the meadows where I used to chase butterflies as a child. They were solidly in houses, and the closest approximation to a butterfly was a tattered Kleenex blowing from a trash can.

In another forty years which butterflies will still be here? Will the variety of species remaining still be a common pleasant sight, or will even a cabbage butterfly be a surprise?

What went wrong? Who is to be blamed? We all are the prime disturbers of our environment to such a degree that the original predator-prey balance has been in places irretrievably lost. In our efforts to build a better life for ourselves wherever we go, we have followed Will Rogers's advice: "Buy land, they ain't makin' it any more," bulldozed the fields and meadows for homes, agriculture, and for industrial development—all in the name of progress. We overdid our mandate: "Be fruitful and increase, fill the earth and subdue it, rule over the fishes in the sea, the birds of the heaven, and every living thing that moves upon the earth." Like the owners of a growth stock we have followed the axiom "Grab ye a profit while ye may," borrowing too optimistically on the future.

In his column "The View from the Castle" in the *Smithsonian Magazine*, the Smithsonian's Secretary, Mr. S. Dillon Ripley, stated:

Endangered species are disappearing at an accelerating rate: Perhaps a million more of our planet's evolved forms of life will become extinct before the century is out.

For too long we have thought that conservation was merely akin to religious fervor, valid as that may be. But in our materialistic society, conservation, like religion, lacks clout. As the Yale biologist Evelyn Hutchinson pointed out, eroding the diversity of species (and their habitats) is economically prodigal. It closes off Man's options and it removes tools a scientist needs to serve humanity.

If endangered species and their habitats, like the air we breathe and the water we drink, can be thought of as common resources of mankind, then they, too, can serve to illuminate other dimensions of the complexities of common property resources.

Just a few years ago this thought would have been looked upon as too drastic, as a doomsday prediction. Today the need to preserve the genetic material of threatened species is very real. Some time ago I participated in a Senate hearing concerning endangered species when I provided audio-visual material in support of the National Museum of Natural History's quest for funds.

One of the questions raised was why it was so important to protect a few wild species of corn growing in some remote areas in Mexico. Dr. Edward S. Ayensu, Director of the Endangered Flora Project at the Smithsonian Institution notes:

If the original parents of corn had become extinct from the wild, we would not have this very important staple today. In fact we can say the same thing for all the

20

13. Nymphalidae: *Anartia jatrophae,* Brazil. This delicate little butterfly is found as far north as southern Florida, where it frequents open meadows, especially if there is a brook or stream nearby.

major crop plants of the world today—they are all the result of hybridization from different varieties. We never know when infectious diseases or altered environmental conditions may one day make it imperative that we return to the wild to draw on the genetic material inherent in plants.

And so it is with all our endangered species, of which butterflies are a part. Lifeless butterflies of all known species and some which are extinct are well-represented in our museum collections, but we know so little still of their lives and behavior. States Dr. Michael Emsley:

In a brain the size of a pinhead there are timers, stimulators, regulators, inhibitors, and coordinators of lives that are rich in maternal preparation, and gourmet delight.

But, he continues:

We do not know how a butterfly works. We do not know how an egg becomes first a caterpillar, then a chrysalis, and then a butterfly—only that it does. Now and then we gain a little insight, but no more than you would of a hotel kitchen by looking in the doorway as the waiters pass in and out.

Watching the behavior of butterflies, one becomes more aware of their place in nature's scheme. If we are to understand their role we must make efforts to learn more about their life cycles, their behavior, their dependence on food plants, and the influence of the predators and parasites in an attempt to find out how the various factors interact to influence the expansion and decline of populations. If even one of the lowly species of butterfly becomes extinct, a new heaven and a new earth must come to pass to create it again. I have an abiding faith in our ability to rise to these challenges to protect our fellow travelers in the ark and reverse these long-range trends. Perhaps it will one day be possible to preserve areas having specific foodplants and rear endangered species of butterflies in the wild. I hope this book will be a small voice of concern for the shrinking habitats of one of nature's great charmers. I also hope that the new trend to prevail among young naturalists will be to shoot the butterfly with the camera lens rather than to capture it with a net.

A book of this magnitude would not have been possible without the cooperative efforts of many persons during the many years it has been in progress. I am very grateful for the encouragement and for the knowledge I have received from my many friends in the National Museum of Natural History, Smithsonian Institution. Here I learned to photograph the hard way, through thousands of trials and many errors. I have always treasured my time in this venerable institution. What started out as a short visit fifteen years ago to obtain material for an encyclopedia of natural history now finds me completely absorbed and interested in animal behavior. Today I produce motion pictures of live biological phenomena for the scientific community in the National Museum of Natural History, Smithsonian Institution.

First of all I will thank my good friend and helper Barbara Bedette for all her assistance and encouragement.

I extend my gratitude to the publishers for their patience and valuable suggestions, particularly to my friends Harry N. Abrams, Fritz Landshoff, and Margaret L. Kaplan of Harry N. Abrams, Inc. (who published my first encyclopedia eighteen years ago). Mention should also be made of Bitita Vinklers, for her capable editing of the text; Ruth Eisenstein and Ann Goedde, who completed preparation of the manuscript for publication; and Dirk Luykx, for his skillful and imaginative design.

A special thanks to my many helpers in the field, who enabled me to photograph many rare specimens in faraway places. Some of the specimens have never been photographed before, and on occasion my photographs were of species new to science. I owe an immeasurable debt of gratitude to the following persons:

Dr. Soernatono Adisoemarto, *Lembaga Biologi Nasional, Indonesia*
Dr. Donald M. Anderson, *USDA, Washington, D.C.*
Dr. Edward S. Ayensu, *Smithsonian Institution*
Dr. Graziela M. Barron, *Jardim Botanico do Rio de Janeiro*
Dr. Graziela Maciel Barroso, *Ins. Brasiliero de desenv., Florestal*

Drs. Roger and Ookeow Beaver, *Chian Mai University, Thailand*

Professor Clifford O. Berg, *Cornell University*

Dr. William M. Briggs, *Victoria University of Wellington, New Zealand*

Dr. Roberto Burle-Marx, *Rio de Janeiro*

Professor Charles E. Cutress, *University of Puerto Rico*

Dr. Donald R. Davis, *Smithsonian Institution*

Dr. Robert L. Dressler, *Smithsonian Tropical Research Institute, Canal Zone*

Dr. W. Donald Duckworth, *Smithsonian Institution*

John Ede, *Mandai Orchid Gardens, Singapore*

Professor Michael Emsley, *George Mason University*

Professor Howard E. Evans, *Colorado State University*

Dr. Graham Bell Fairchild, *Panama City*

Dr. Italo Claudio Falesi, *IPEAN, Belém, Brazil*

William D. Field, *Smithsonian Institution*

Dr. Richard C. Froeschner, *Smithsonian Institution*

Dr. Robert D. Gordon, *USDA, Washington, D.C.*

Francis M. Greenwell, *Smithsonian Institution*

Dr. J. Linsley Gressitt, *Wau Ecology Institute, New Guinea*

Dr. M. P. Harris, *Galapagos Islands*

Dr. Porter M. Kier, *Smithsonian Institution*

Dr. Lloyd V. Knutson, *USDA, Washington, D.C.*

Professor Kenneth P. Lamb, *University of Papua and New Guinea*

Dr. Vincente H. F. Morses, *IPEAN, Belém, Brazil*

Professor Martin Naumann, *University of Connecticut*

Dr. Joao Murca Pires, *IPEAN, Belém, Brazil*

Dr. Ivan Polunin, *University of Singapore*

Dr. Ghillean T. Prance, *INPA, Manaus, Brazil*

Professor Diomedes Quintero, *Universidad de Panama*

Dr. Amada A. Reimer, *Smithsonian Tropical Research Institute, Canal Zone*

Dr. Raulino Reitz, *Jardim Botanico do Rio de Janeiro*

Dr. Curtis W. Sabrosky, *USDA, Washington, D.C.*

Professor Margot Schumm, *Montgomery Community College, Maryland*

Professor Laura Schuster, *Universidad A. de la Selva, Peru*

Professor Nicolas Smythe, *University of Costa Rica*

Dr. Thomas R. Soderstrom, *Smithsonian Institution*

Dr. Paul J. Spangler, *Smithsonian Institution*

Rose Ella Warner Spilman, *USDA, Washington, D.C.*

T. J. Spilman, *USDA, Washington, D.C.*

George C. Steyskal, *USDA, Washington, D.C.*

Dr. Alcides R. Teixeira, *Instituto de Botanico, São Paulo*

Richard Thacker, *University of Maryland*

Dr. Edward L. Todd, *USDA, Washington, D.C.*

Dr. Cesar Mazabel Torres, *Universidad A. de la Selva, Peru*

Professor Roman Vishniac, *Yeshiva University*

Professor Thomas J. Walker, *University of Florida*

David Wapinsky, *University of Virginia*

Kirsten Wegener-Kofoed, *Copenhagen, Denmark*
J. S. Womersley, *Lae Botanical Gardens, New Guinea*
Choo See Yan Brothers, *Cameron Highlands, Malaysia*
Professor Fernandez Yepez, *University of Maracay, Venezuela*

Kjell B. Sandved
*National Museum of Natural History*
*Smithsonian Institution, Washington, D.C.*

# ACKNOWLEDGMENTS

A book is never the work of one person alone. The present volume has been made possible only with the generously given expertise of many people in many different fields. I would particularly like to express my gratitude to the following:

The staff of the Reference Department of the Newton Free Library, especially Mrs. Margaret Snyder.

The staff of the Classical Department of the Boston Museum of Fine Arts, especially Dr. Cornelius Vermeule, Curator.

The staff of the Department of Entomology of the National Museum of Natural History of the Smithsonian Institution, and especially Dr. J. F. Gates Clarke, for help in the identification of very difficult species, and Dr. Don R. Davis for six photographs of an Incurvariid moth taken under the electron microscope.

George F. Brewer, my late husband, for help in all matters involving logistics.

Dr. Howard Ensign Evans, Colorado State University, Dr. John M. Burns and Dr. Robert Silberglied, Harvard University, and Stanley S. Nicolay for many assists, both great and small.

Dr. Frank Morton Carpenter, Harvard University, for a photograph of the fossil butterfly *Prodryas persephone.*

Anna Maria Abernathy, Newton, Massachusetts, for translations from the German.

Stephen Grohe, Boston, for translation of 35 mm slides into the black-and-white plates.

Jo Brewer
*Founding Associate Director, Xerces Society*
*Auburndale, Massachusetts*

14. *right:* Nymphalidae: *Hypolimnas misippus,* West Afr[i] This is the male of the species. [T] wings on the dorsal side are iridescent purple with large whi[te] spots, but the female is a nearl[y] perfect mimic of *Danaus chrysippus.*

*Overleaf:*
15. Riodinidae: *Cartea vitula,* Brazil. All butterflies with this coloring and pattern are protec[ted] to some extent from bird predators, whether they are poisonous butterflies or not.

16. *inset far left:* Nymphalidae: *Adelpha iphicla,* Trinidad. The white band, similar to those on wings of many other butterflies[,] disruptive, serving to disguise t[he] actual shape of the wings, especially if the butterfly is res[ting] in sun-dappled woods.

17. *inset left:* Pieridae, Brazil. A large congregation of Pierid butterflies, and one *Dryas julia* (family Heliconiidae), drinking f[rom] damp sand near a pool of water[.] This phenomenon has often bee[n] observed, especially among th[e] Pieridae and the Papilionidae. T[he] "puddle clubs" seem to be exclusively male. The butterflie[s] drink avidly and excrete a drop [of] clear fluid about every ten secon[ds.] The function of this ritual is no[t] clearly understood.

18. *inset right:* Papilionidae: *Trogonoptera brookiana,* Borne[o.] One of the exotic birdwing butterflies, here drinking from damp sand. It is an unusually la[rge] butterfly, with a wing span up t[o] 7½". An enlargement of its fore[-] wing appears in plate 213.

19. *inset far right:* Riodinidae: *Chalodeta, sp.,* British Hondura[s.] Butterflies of this family are ca[lled] metal marks because of the bri[ght] metallic spots on their wings.

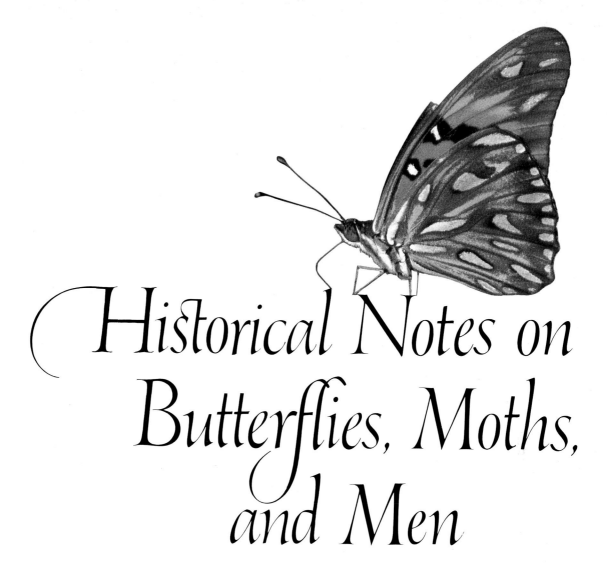

# Historical Notes on Butterflies, Moths, and Men

In approaching the study of butterflies, one is always faced with a dilemma. Should they be considered as an aspect of science to be scrutinized, subjected to experimentation, and solved; or should they be looked upon as something purely aesthetic—food for the spirit, better left unhampered by factual complications? Linnaeus, the great Swedish botanist of the eighteenth century, seems to have taken the former view. He classified not only butterflies, but all animals and plants known to him, according to his own taxonomic system, giving each a generic and a specific name. His system has been in a state of flux ever since, with his successors subdividing and sorting it, in an effort to find in the relationships among species the key to their evolutionary beginnings.

The Oriental poets and philosophers, it seems, have taken the aesthetic view. Butterflies are the subject of many beautiful Chinese legends, stories, and philosophical arguments. In Japanese haiku they become the most delicate of symbols:

*The Flower Wreath*
Butterflies love and
Follow the flower wreath that
On the coffin lies.
MEISETSU

*Untitled Haiku*
A garden butterfly;
The baby crawls, it flies . . .
She crawls, it flies . . .
ISSA

In the synthetic, cacophonic, electronic wonderworld of the twentieth century, such choices are still made by the scientist and the poet-philosopher but, between these two, there is a vast population, trapped in a world of withering roots and disappearing greenery, that is forced to contend with and have faith in a technological monolith it cannot fully understand, and made to confront a proliferation of plastic trivia. Beauty in its most profound sense is becoming a rarity, and therefore increasingly valuable. The natural wonders that people took for granted a century ago they must now fight to retain.

Patronage of the arts has traditionally fallen to the wealthy, the knowledgeable, the connoisseurs. Natural beauty belongs to everyone, rich or poor, scholar or politician, poet or scientist. And natural beauty is, after all, the highest form of art—the perfect art from which all other forms have sprung. Butterflies, small, ephemeral, glittering with life and color, are the Chinese ivories, the Limoges enamels, the Renaissance jewelry—the artistic miniatures of the living world, worthy to be both understood and admired.

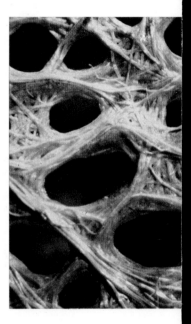

The science of butterflies is neither dull nor dogmatic. It is like the unfolding of a mystery, the ending of which is not known until the last page is turned. It is much more than a detailed knowledge of taxonomy, which, for the majority of people, is not relevant to what they see or how they live. What is relevant is an appreciation of the consummate beauty of a living butterfly, and an understanding of both its fragility and its tenacity.

Until fifty years ago, butterflies had managed to survive evolution without serious loss. Today they are on trial. The criterion of their worth is their aesthetic value; their chance of survival, our awareness of it. This book is written in the hope of furthering such an awareness. It is not written for the dedicated professional who is already aware of nature's magnificence and the forces which threaten it. Perhaps it may find its way into the consciousness of those who now encounter the natural world, seeing nothing in it worth saving. But, principally, it is intended as a meeting ground for those who have learned too little or too much to love, and those who love too much to destroy. It is for the lover of beauty, whose enjoyment is made deeper by the exploration of life's mysteries, always within the framework of life's resplendence. To these, whoever you are, wherever you are, this book is dedicated.

In numbers of species, the Lepidoptera constitute the second largest order in the animal world. Over the face of the earth, about 135,000 species of butterflies and moths are known to exist. Roughly 111,000 of these species are moths, only about 24,000 butterflies. But butterflies fly in the daylight, especially on the warmest and most shining of days, when all the most pleasing facets of nature seem to be marshaled to provide a background for them. Perhaps, because of this idyllic setting, and also because butterflies themselves are so breathtakingly beautiful, they have gained a special status. From people the world over, they elicit responses of admiration, wonder, and delight accorded to no other insect. They spark the imagination of poet and artist alike, and have come to be a reflection of man's search for Nirvana—for those things which are beyond human grasp.

Moths usually hide themselves during the day, flying only at night or in the early evening. A very large majority of them have never been seen alive by anyone excepting the entomologists who seek them out. Some are attracted to light at night, and are familiar to us as dim and dusky forms fluttering like ghosts against windows or around lamps. For hundreds of years, moths were regarded as night-time butterflies, and no other difference between the two was recognized. Both moths and butterflies were called psychae by the ancient Greeks.

In Latin, the word *papilio* is generally understood to mean "butterfly." However, the Latin language also includes the word *blatta* (creatures that fly in the night)—a word which could indicate moths, but is also applied to cockroaches and other nocturnal creatures. But Pliny the Elder, who was the natural-history expert of his time, defined *papilio* as "a cowardly and ignoble creature that flutters up to lamps when they are lit, and is destructive and inimical to bees; not in one way only, for [it] eats the wax and also leaves excrement in which worms are produced which attack the wax."

The *papilio* described here by Pliny must have been a moth, since moths, not butterflies, habitually flutter up to lamps. Ovid, in his *Metamorphoses*, also used the word *papilio*: "And worms that weave their white cocoons on the leaves of trees (a fact well known to country folk) change into funereal butterflies."

Ovid was doubtless referring to the Greek idea that the soul left the body in the form of a butterfly; but since moths, not butterflies, spin cocoons, *papilione* should also mean "moth" here. However, the false idea that butterflies spin cocoons, far from being dispelled today, has been so often repeated that it is now tolerated as poetic license. Thus the confusion on this particular point will probably continue in the minds of people as long as moths and butterflies remain on earth and poetry is written about them. Both butterflies and moths change from caterpillars to pupae. The pupa of a butterfly is commonly called a chrysalis, and usually hangs head down from a button of silk or is attached to the underside of a twig or to some flat surface by a silken belt. The pupa of a moth is usually buried in the ground or encased in a silken shell. This silken shell is a cocoon (plate 21).

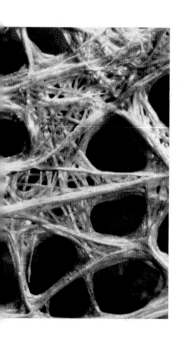

21. Detail of the cocoon spun by a Javanese Saturnid caterpillar. A cocoon is the silken covering spun by the caterpillar of some moths to protect themselves during the pupal stage. Attempts have been made to use the silk of various Saturnid moths for the manufacture of silken fabrics, but only *Bombyx mori* (family Bombycidae) produces silk strong enough to be commercially valuable.

Taken as a class, insects have not been numbered among the friends of man. They have infected him with diseases which sap his strength and decimate his ranks. They have destroyed his crops, undermined his houses, damaged his clothing—and even his books. They mar his enjoyment of life by biting and stinging his flesh. Too small and too numerous to be hunted and overcome like other animals, they are looked upon with distrust, even fear, and in either case, as something to be exterminated.

The ancient Hebrews were experts in the control of clothes moths, for it was of prime importance for them to preserve the costly garments of fine light wool which constituted their wardrobes. In ancient Hebrew writings, moths appear as symbols of destruction: "The moth shall consume them like a garment and the worm shall eat them like wool" (Isaiah 51:8). The Hebrews had two words for moth, *ash* and *sas,* but there was no word for butterfly in their

33

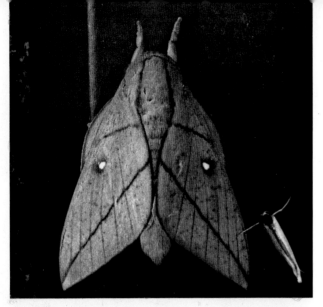

22. Moth resting with wings folded back against its body.

# HOW BUTTERFLIES DIFFER FROM MOTHS

Moths and butterflies differ in a number of habits, chief among them being the manner in which they hold their wings. When moths are at rest, they usually lie flat against the bark of a tree or some other surface which camouflages them, with their fore wings covering their hind wings. Butterflies at rest fold their wings over their backs.

There are also certain physiological differences between the two insects. The bodies of moths tend to be larger in relation to the wings than the bodies of butterflies. Some moths have no mechanism for drinking, whereas all butterflies do. Some moths

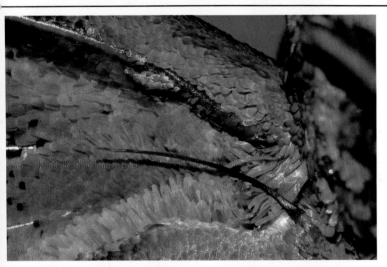

24. Castniidae, Brazil. The frenulum on the underside of the hind wings of a moth, holding the fore wing and hind wing together in flight. Butterfly wings, in most species, are held together by a flap on the upper margin of the hind wing.

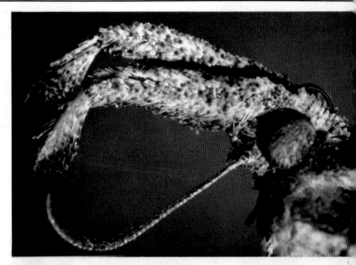

25. Noctuidae, United States. The males of some species of Noctuidae have exceptionally long palpi. This plate shows the head, greatly magnified, of a moth measuring less than an inch from wing tip to wing tip. It is thought that the palpi of moths and butterflies were originally legs and that over millions of years they have migrated to the insect's head and developed into organs related to scent perception.

28. *above:* Saturniidae. Moths of the family Saturniidae have antennae which are feathery, or fernlike. This antenna belongs to a European Saturnid.

29. *above right:* Sphingidae. Tip of the antenna of a European sphinx moth, slightly swollen at the end.

30. *right:* Sphingidae, India. Tip of the antenna of a sphinx moth, swollen, hooked, and tapering.

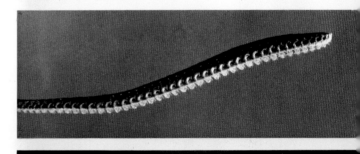

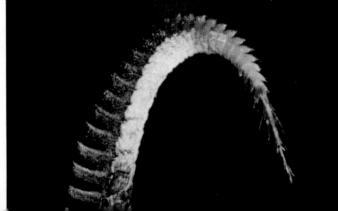

have a device, the frenulum, which hooks their fore wings to their hind wings in flight. Butterflies never do.

In most species, a diagnosis can be made by the antennae. Moth antennae are either plain and tapering or fernlike. Those of butterflies are knobbed at the end, hence the name Rhopalocera (club-ended) for the suborder of butterflies. Such rules are broad and general, with enough exceptions to confound all but the experts. They are mentioned here in the hope that they may clarify rather than confuse.

The moths most frequently seen are rather small and drab, giving rise to the belief that moths are not as beautiful as butterflies. This spectrum of moths, chosen at random from a host of equally colorful tropical and subtropical species, may help to dispel that belief.

23. Butterfly resting with closed wings.

26. Riodinidae: *Anteros carausius,* Mexico. Underside view. Two of the characteristics that distinguish this small butterfly from a moth are clearly shown here. The antennae are clubbed at the ends, and a rounded flap at the costal edge of the hind wing keeps it behind the fore wing in flight.

27. A Saturnid moth, with fernlike antennae. Its wings are in resting position.

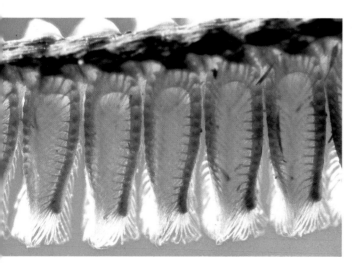

31. Sphingidae, Mexico. Detail of sensory hairs on the underside of the antenna of a sphinx moth.

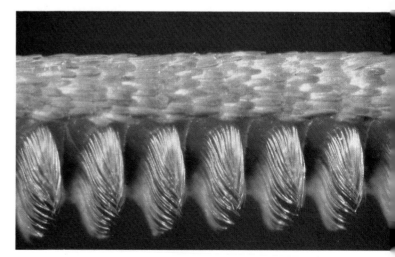

32. Sphingidae, Australia. Detail of sensory hairs on the underside of the antenna of a sphinx moth of the genus *Metamimus,* greatly enlarged. The tufts of hairs at the base and tip make the antennae of Sphingidae unlike those of any other family of moths.

33. *left:* Pericopidae, Venezuela.

34. *above:* Arctiidae, Venezuela. In the family Arctiidae, the caterpillars have all four pairs of abdominal prolegs and are thickly covered with furry hair. In this stage some of them are popularly called woolly bears. They shed this hair before pupating and incorporate it into their cocoons as they spin. The wings of the moths are often colorful. Keats describes Madeline's window in "The Eve of St. Agnes" as "diamonded with panes of quaint device,/ Innumerable of stains and splendid dyes / As are the tiger-moth's deep-damask'd wings."

35. *below left:* Ctenuchidae, Venezuela.

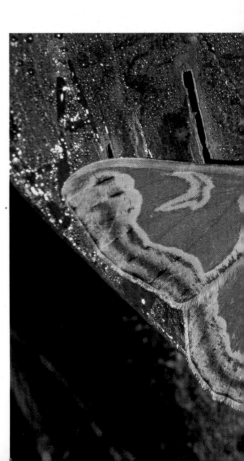

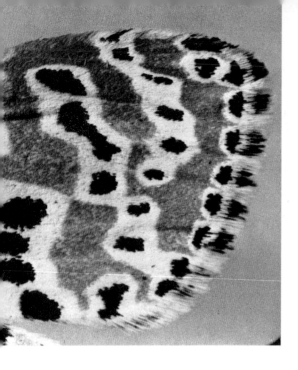

36. *above:* Arctiidae, Cuba. Detail of a wing.

37. *above right:* Noctuidae, Brazil. Contrary to the common belief that moths are dull in comparison to butterflies, there is no end to the variety in moth patterns and colors. Of the three families, the Noctuidae (plate 37) are the least colorful overall but the most cryptic in appearance, depending on camouflage to conceal themselves during the day and when flying by night. Their species number in the thousands. By contrast the Pericopidae (plate 33) are few but gaudy, and in South America may belong to a mimicry complex. The Arctiidae (plate 38), another large family, are known as tiger moths because of their bright colors and beautiful, often striped, patterns.

38. *right:* Arctiidae, Brazil.

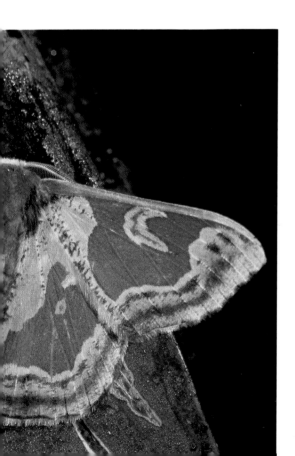

39. *left:* Geometridae, Guatemala. The Geometridae are another very large moth family. Geometrids occur in the world wherever green things are growing. The caterpillars are long and thin, often resembling twigs to a remarkable degree. They have only one pair of walking prolegs, whereas most caterpillars have four. As a result they must hitch themselves along by alternately drawing the rear legs up close to the thorax and stretching the body out to its full length. In the process the middle part of the body forms a loop. These repeated contortions have earned the caterpillars the name "inch worms," or "loopers." In relation to the size of the body, the wings are larger than those of most moths, and the Geometridae, an exception to the general rule, fly during the day or at dusk rather than at night. The females are usually wingless and often differ so greatly from the males that no one seeing them for the first time would believe they were of the same species.

language until the year 1900, when *porpor* was first included in the dictionary of Ben Yehudah.

Yet, certain insects have been used by man to great advantage. John the Baptist is reported to have lived upon locusts and wild honey while he was in the desert. The locusts he ate were probably not the seeds of the locust tree, as has been suggested, but insects. The latter theory is given credence by the fact that the locust was—and is—a common pest in the Middle East, and also by the fact that some insects, including grubs, termites, locusts, and grasshoppers, have always been staple food sources in many areas of the world. The revulsion toward eating insects seems to be a product of modern civilization, based upon emotion rather than reason. When a moth or butterfly larva has just pupated, it is pure protein, very nutritious, and cleaner than the lobster or crab, to which it is not very distantly related. Agave "worms," a delicacy to be found in the United States only in the more exotic food stores, but a staple food in Mexico, are the caterpillars of a large skipper butterfly of the genus *Megathymus*.

The two insect products most valued by man are honey and silk, and consequently bees and silkworms have become domesticated creatures. Domestic bees live in a semicaptive state. They are free to fly, but their activities are controlled. Silkworms seldom reach maturity, apart from those which are allowed to become moths in order to mate and replenish the colony. Otherwise, the cocoons are boiled before the silk is unwound. In ancient China, the cocoon shells which remained after the silk had been removed were cracked open like almonds and the larvae eaten. The same practice may be in effect today, a fringe benefit to workers in the silk industry.

Both the ladybug and the praying mantis are sold in large numbers to gardeners and farmers for use in controlling insect pests, and the cochineal, a scale insect, provides a red dye sometimes used as a food coloring.

Besides these "domesticated" insects, the earth under our feet abounds with small creatures which exist unseen, living, feeding, mating, and dying beneath the grass. They aerate the soil with their tunneling and enrich it with their excrement. Also caterpillars return to the earth waste products rich in soil nutrients.

Although butterflies played a definite role in the life, art, and symbolism of the Egyptian and Minoan cultures, they seem not to have been important to other Middle Eastern peoples. Possibly in many of these areas, with their miles of arid plateau and desert, butterflies were relatively scarce. But the Nile cuts a green swath through the sands of Egypt, and along its marshy banks there was and is an abundance of waterfowl and butterflies. The jungles of Africa, south of the Sahara, are the home of over 2,400 species, including some of the world's most exotic butterflies, but in the desert itself they are absent.

Lavish growth and hot damp climate make an ideal condition for butterflies. Mexico has for many centuries been the home of numerous species, and their presence is reflected in the art, architecture, and folklore from the earliest known tribes to the destruction of Pre-Columbian civilization. Over 700 species of butterflies are native to the rain forests and jungles of Brazil. In the Malay-

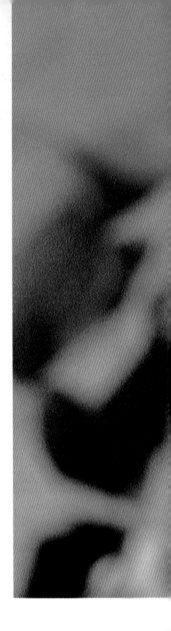

40. Heliconiidae: *Agraulis vanil* A tropical butterfly also occurrir in the United States (Florida an California). It is a fast flyer and frequent visitor of flowers—her is shown drinking from one. The female lays her eggs on the passion vine, a poisonous plant and this causes the butterfly to poisonous. Hence it is warningly colored.

38

sian tropics there are nearly 1,000 species. In the little principality of Sikkim, near India, there was a variety and abundance of butterflies so magnificent as to be unsurpassed anywhere else in the world until a few years ago, when massive spraying for control of the malaria mosquito decimated their numbers. No one would argue against exterminating the malaria mosquito, but there are many who deplore this method of accomplishing it, attended by the callous sacrifice of other creatures which are neither destructive nor harmful. Butterflies themselves, in the adult winged state, fall into this category.

In fact, they have even made a unique contribution to man's welfare. Experiments with the African swallowtail, *Papilio dardanus*, which has several distinct female forms, have revealed that a single gene change causes the difference between one form and another. The similarity of these crossing supergenes in butterflies to the genetic structure in human beings of different blood types led to the development of the anti-RH treatment for the detection of "Rhesus" babies. More recently, under the aegis of the National Cancer Institute, a search has been made for anti-cancer agents present in animals and

plants. It was discovered that the wings of a common little yellow butterfly of
Taiwan (*Catopsilia crocale*) contain a rare substance with promise of being effective. A quarter of a million butterflies were collected to obtain enough of the
drug for initial experiments and for possibly making a synthetic substance. It
has been used on laboratory rats and has a very encouraging anti-tumor effect.

Butterflies prey upon no other creature, and they cause no damage to
anything valued by man. Perhaps this very neutrality is the reason why they
have so often been used to symbolize the things of the spirit. Even the brief
exploratory pauses in their seemingly undirected flight suggest a lack of interest in material things. They maintain an easy state of symbiosis within their
own world, pollinating the flowers from which they take nectar. And, since
the flowers they prefer are wild flowers of the field, intrinsic benefits to mankind from this activity are minimal. Indeed, any advantage to man, any contribution to science, any gift to the earth made by a butterfly must remain
secondary to the perfect and defenseless beauty of it flashing in air, becoming
suddenly poised on a blossom, being absorbed in the act of drinking, or slowly
opening and closing its marvelous wings. It is for this that we pay our toll of
an unsprayed tree, an undisturbed patch of thistle, or an uncut plot of meadow
grass on which a few small caterpillars may be allowed to wander and grow as
they live out the two weeks of their short life.

# Butterflies in Art, Heraldry, and Religion

The history of butterflies in art—and, since art and symbolism cannot be separated—also in symbolism, is a fascinating one. In art butterflies have appeared since the cradle days of civilization. As symbols, their meaning has changed from one era to another (a kind of metamorphosis not uncommon to symbolism) according to the mores, religious beliefs, and folklore of the times.

In tomb paintings and sculptures of ancient Egypt (plate 42), they are frequently found in scenes along the banks of the Nile, and so were included among the pleasures to be encountered by the dead, who in the afterworld enjoyed the popular occupation of fowling in the marshes.

Butterflies, other than those in fowling scenes, are exceedingly rare among the cultural remains of ancient Egypt. They seem to have played a much more important role in contemporaneous Mycenae, where a surprising number, mostly gold ornaments, have been unearthed. In one undisturbed grave was found the body of a young woman which had been clothed in a tunic of gold discs. Various designs, including butterflies, were stamped into these discs, as seals are pressed into paper, suggesting that they were not unique but "mass produced," and perhaps frequently used in burials. Other artifacts and jewelry found at Mycenae give evidence that the butterfly had some religious significance for these early people. In any case, it was surely considered a thing of beauty, and its metamorphosis was at least partly understood, for golden chrysalids as well as golden butterflies have been found.

In the religion of ancient Greece, the first recorded accounts describe souls of the dead as fluttering away to the underworld, unwillingly but without resisting, to return no more. In later thinking, the soul could reappear— even come and go—in the form of a small moth or butterfly. This concept was still expressed in the late Roman period, on funerary sculpture now lost but fortunately made immortal by an Italian scholar named Dal Pozzo (plate 43). Beginning shortly after 1600, with several hired artists, he made drawings of all the sculpture and statuary which existed in Rome at that time. In a very few of these—probably less than half a dozen—a butterfly can be found, symbolizing the soul of the departed. This idea may be credited to Aristotle, who, in the fourth century B.C., first used the word "psyche" to mean both soul and butterfly.

The legend of Cupid and Psyche probably originated long before the time of Aristotle, but it was not put into writing, so far as is known, until the second century A.D. by Apuleius. According to his story in *The Golden Ass,* Cupid, son of Venus, fell in love with the beautiful young girl Psyche, and she with him. Every night he flew to earth and the two spent the hours of darkness in ecstatic bliss, wrapped in each other's arms. But Psyche was warned by her lover that she must never look on his face. Of course, Psyche being mortal, curiosity triumphed. Cupid fled, and the heartbroken girl wandered to the ends of the

42. *above:* Limestone frieze from the Tomb of Ka-em-Nofiet at Sakkara, Egypt. 2450 B.C., Old Kingdom, Fifth Dynasty. Museum of Fine Arts, Boston. Birds occupy most of this frieze, but the enormous size of the one butterfly seems to give it unusual importance. Similar butterflies have been found in other tombs the same period at Sakkara.

43. *left:* Cavaliere Cassiano dal Pozzo. Drawing of a bas-relief on late Roman cinerarium, now lost. Early seventeenth century. The Royal Library in Windsor Castle. mourning woman points downward, signifying death. A godlike figure, possibly Prometheus, holds a soul in the form of a butterfly. A dead child's portrait is encircled above it.

44. *right: Winged Psyche.* Roman fourth century B.C., probably copied from a Greek original, now lost. Marble. Capitoline Museum, Rome Wings are rarely found on life-size statues of Psyche such as this; small statuettes usually have wings similar to those of a damsel fly.

earth vainly seeking her lost love. Finally Jupiter took pity on her, rendered her immortal, and the lovers were reunited to live forever among the gods. Thus Psyche achieved a dual personality. She became recognized not only as the image of the immortal soul, but also as the symbol of the anguish and triumph of love.

Apuleius did not describe her as winged, but this concept must have been well established in his day, for Psyche had been represented with wings since the time of Aristotle. On various Roman sarcophagi the soul, in the form of Psyche with butterfly wings, is seen leaving the body of the dead (plate 44).

Roman gemstones show her in her other guise—that of a lovelorn maiden —where she is usually symbolized by a butterfly being burned by Cupid. Psyche, as the symbol of love's anguish, became a popular theme. It was expressed by Charles, Duc d'Orléans, who spent his time writing poetry while he was held captive in England in the fifteenth century. He was expressing regret for lost love when he included this line in a rondel: "I burned me at the candle, as doth the butterfly." A similar approach to love frequently appears in the Emblemata books of the sixteenth century. An emblem from the book of Claude Paradin (Antwerp, 1562) shows a butterfly flying into a candle flame with the motto: "*Così vivo piacer Conduce a Morte*" (Thus too lively pleasure leads to death). This and several similar emblems of the same era are elaborated in a popular rhyme of the day:

> In moderation, love is praised and prized.
> Death and dishonor in excess it brings.
> In burning warmth, how fail its boasted wings,
> As simple butterflies in light chastized.

Raphael was probably the most famous painter to use the Cupid and Psyche theme. He decorated the summer palace of Agostino Chigi in Rome with the legend according to Apuleius, but added a wedding banquet scene. Psyche has lost her butterfly wings in these frescos, but they are being worn by beneficent sprites fluttering above the heads of the happy couple.

Oddly enough, in the Victorian era Psyche suddenly became a symbol of purity. Winged once more, and nude to the waist, she was used as a trademark for Poland Spring Water! Today the butterfly is embraced by the youth culture, not as a symbol of love and pain, but of love and peace. But it also retains its erotic and religious implications—the two faces of Psyche. A monarch butterfly appeared painted on the thigh of the youthful heroine in the motion picture *I Love You, Alice B. Toklas.* In the Swedish motion picture *Elvira Madigan* the heroine releases a white butterfly from between her palms at the moment when she is shot by her lover.

The earliest known major work of art of the Christian era on which a butterfly appears is the Chalice of Antioch (plate 45). The insect is small and mothlike, and may indeed be a moth, but since both moths and butterflies were "psychae" and since the difference between them was not recognized until much later, they must be regarded as one and the same at this period and for many centuries following.

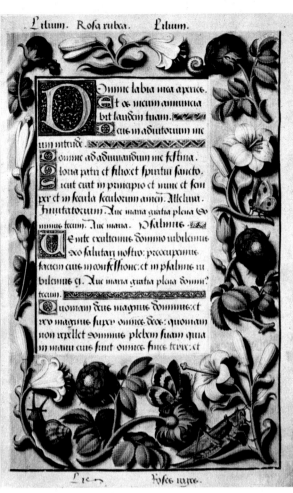

After the fall of Rome, butterflies in both art and symbolism virtually disappeared from the Western world until late in the Middle Ages. This was partly because the hierarchy, at the Council of Nicaea (325), had set down stringent rules for the use of ornament in the Christian church, and because, at the same period, interest in nature and science was being stifled by a proliferation of superstitions, religious and otherwise.

During the early Middle Ages, when the accumulated knowledge of thousands of years had not yet been rediscovered, the vast majority of people, in the absence of any real intellectual stimulus, had turned to the supernatural as a way of thought. Anything could be an omen, however small—a fly alighting on one's cheek, a mouse twitching its whiskers, a butterfly or moth coming in through a window. Butterflies were souls, not only of people, but of other living things as well. For example, in some areas, if a butterfly or moth was seen fluttering over a field of grain, it was interpreted as a sign that the grain had lost its soul, and elaborate measures had to be taken to restore it in order to save the crop.

In the art of the late Middle Ages and early Renaissance, butterflies are occasionally found in works commissioned by individuals for their own use.

45. *above far left:* The Chalice of Antioch, found near Antioch, Syria Fourth, possibly fifth, century. Silver, partially gilt, height 7½", diameter 6". Metropolitan Museum of Art, New York (The Cloisters Collection, Purchase 1950). Surrounded by a grapevine (symbol of life), sits a man, possibly an apostle, his hand almost touching a butterfly or moth. Above his head a locust rests on the vine.

46. *above left:* Jean Bourdichon. *Hours of the Virgin.* Early sixteenth century, illuminated manuscript. The Pierpont Morgan Library, New York. Roses and lilies, the flowers most closely associated with the Virgin, are combined with butterflies, symbols of resurrection, and a locust, symbol of destruction. Text includes *Gloria Patri* and *Ave Maria.*

44

The Apocalypse tapestries, woven about 1379 in the shop of Nicolas Bataille,
are an example. Butterflies decorate the background of three panels in which
great men sit enthroned. In the remains of the Nine Heroes tapestry at the
Cloisters in New York, also the work of Bataille, the same butterflies appear
along the edges of two panels. Bataille may have used them as a sort of trademark.

Butterflies began to be used in the borders of illuminated manuscripts,
especially the Book of Hours and the Breviary, early in the fourteenth century
(plate 46). Several years were often required to make these exquisite volumes,
which were prized possessions of both men and women of the nobility—prized
not only because of their religious content, but equally as works of art. Butterflies increased in favor as border decorations as time went on and reached the
peak of their popularity in the works of the famous French miniaturist Jehan
Bourdichon, in the early sixteenth century. In some books, butterflies were
used in conjunction with other familiar symbols, leaving no doubt that the
entire border was intended to reflect the content of the central subject. In other
instances, the borders appear to be merely decorative.

In Italian painting of the Middle Ages and the Renaissance, butterflies

49. Grave monument. Nineteenth century. Wolfsgottesacher, Basel. The butterfly flies above its own caterpillar, symbolizing the resurrection of the soul. The quotation from Luke reads: "For h is not a God of the dead, but of th living: for all live unto him." The carefully sculptured caterpillar ha four pairs of prolegs and three pairs of true legs.

are exceedingly rare. However, the Veronese artist Pisanello (c. 1380–1451) painted a charming profile of a young girl, elegantly clothed and coiffed, her calm, pensive expression in sharp contrast to a background of windblown flowers and butterflies, all beautifully executed, and of recognizable species (plate 47).

The first artist to use butterflies in a painting of the Madonna seems to have been Albrecht Dürer (1471–1528). In his *Adoration of the Magi* in the Uffizi Gallery, two familiar species, the painted lady (*Vanessa cardui*) and a female of the clouded yellow (*Colias crocea*) rest unobtrusively in the lower left corner. These may well have been intended as symbols. Dürer was noted for his interest in mystic signs and hidden symbols, which appear frequently in his engravings. He introduced several butterflies into engravings of the Madonna in conjunction with other symbols of life and death.

Butterflies really became an important element in artistic composition in the seventeenth century with the rise of the Dutch flower painters. A majority of the bouquets contain at least one or two butterflies, and in some, especially those by Van Huysum, there are many more; there are twenty-two butterflies and moths in one of his paintings, all "portraits" of actual species. One can often find caterpillars, dragon flies, bees, and other insects also. In the Louvre there is an elaborate flower wreath by the Dutch Jesuit painter Brother Daniel Seghers (1590–1661), in which there are six butterflies and one moth, all painted in the most meticulous detail (plate 48). In the center of the wreath, there is a scene called "The Triumph of Love," a strange perversion of the Cupid and Psyche myth. Love is a winged baby cupid riding in a chariot drawn by doves. It is the work of Domenico Zampieri. Seghers painted only flower wreaths; the pictures within the wreaths are by various artists and are nearly always religious in character. Since Seghers was a monk, he never received money for his works, which were usually donated to churches to be used as altarpieces. Apparently a few found their way into the hands of secular art-

50. Grave monument. Nineteenth century. Newton Cemetery, Newton, Mass. This beautiful stor is ornamented with a monarch butterfly just emerged from its chrysalis.

46

51. R. E. Milne. Archway of the
Soldiers' Memorial. Twentieth
century, stone. Ottawa, Canada.
This decorative frieze depicts the
small creatures encountered by
soldiers of the Canadian army
while they were in the trenches
during World War I. Besides the
birds, squirrel, and butterfly, there
are also spiders, rats, and fleas.
The grapevine is a symbol of
everlasting life.

ists, but it seems highly unlikely that Brother Seghers would have been pleased with the fate of the wreath just described.

A rather provocative canvas by Balthasar van der Ast (c. 1590–c. 1656) called *Still Life with Shells* shows the European peacock butterfly (*Nymphalis io*) hovering over a mound of shells. The peacock (for which this butterfly was named) is a symbol of immortality; the empty shell signifies death.

A great surge of interest in classical Greece arose during the nineteenth century following the discovery of the Elgin marbles, which were purchased by the British government in 1816. It is not surprising that the butterfly, as a symbol of the soul separated from the body, found its widest expression in the grass-roots art of tomb sculpture during the Greek revival. Funeral monuments reflect perhaps better than any other artistic medium the tastes, feelings, and religious beliefs of the people. The butterfly theme is said to have been found on Greek tombs and steles no longer extant. It can still be seen, personified by Psyche, on Roman sarcophagi. So far, at least twenty-nine tombs and gravestones on which butterflies are used as symbols of the soul released from the body have been discovered; of these, twenty-one were erected during the nineteenth century (plates 49, 50).

The idea of life after death is reinforced on a number of these stones, by the inclusion of caterpillars or chrysalids as well as butterflies. The hope of life after death in a new form is central to Christianity, but in the tombstones erected during the period of the Greek revival it is also a reflection of the ancient Greek concept of the soul departing from or returning to earth as a butterfly.

In the decorative arts, butterflies abound. The eye of the lepidopterist, attuned to their presence in the field, sees butterflies in embroideries, tapestries, cut glass, laces, dishes, in all the small niches where the unpracticed eye passes over them, seeing only that which is obvious. Three examples will suffice to show the spirit of freedom and gaiety achieved in many such cases.

52. *above:* Philippe Mombaers.
Faïence platter. Eighteenth century.
Musée Communal, Brussels.

53. *left:* Cut-glass pitcher,
American. c. 1909. Collection
Mrs. George Brewer.

In the Musée Communal, Brussels, a collection of plates designed by Philippe Mombaers (active 1724–54), founder of the faïence industry of Brussels, is of particular interest (plate 52). The plates are bordered with the rich copper-green for which Mombaers was famous. Inside the border there is a ring of butterflies, alternating with caterpillars and chrysalids. This pottery is a great rarity, since a single work of art which includes all three of these stages in the metamorphosis cycle of the butterfly is almost unheard of.

In the nineteenth century, John LaFarge designed a butterfly window, now in the Museum of Fine Arts, Boston, which is the essence of summer— light, color, and motion.

Deep-cut glass of the late period was a unique contribution of the early twentieth century (plate 53). Deep-cut glass is decorated by intersecting straight lines. Early designs were geometric, but glass of the late period was cut in such a way that straight lines were transformed into realistic images; form was achieved by length, width, and depth of cut and the angle at which the glass was held. Because of the interplay of reflections, light, and shadow, decorations made in this manner possessed the delicate vibrant quality of real butterflies and flowers, although a pitcher or vase so cut was usually five-eighths of an inch thick and weighed five pounds.

Today, butterflies are being used for the first time in stained-glass windows to symbolize the resurrection of the soul. Sometimes they are associated with subjects such as the raising of the dead; sometimes they are merely included in a succession of symbolic medallions.

Modern designs and embroideries for priestly vestments also include butterflies in their symbolism, and the association of butterflies and flowers in church decorations at Easter is a growing trend. One of the most delightful of modern butterflies appears on a Christmas card designed by Joe Brainard for The Museum of Modern Art in New York. A huge swallowtail in the background gives the Madonna the appearance of having magnificent wings.

Among the artifacts discovered at Minoa were numerous small clay seals which are thought to have been used in securing packages. Why the seals should have been embossed with various designs (including butterflies) is not known, but it has been suggested that they were perhaps family emblems, used to identify the sender of a parcel. If true, this is the earliest use of the butterfly as a personal emblem. During the Greek Classical period many hundreds of years later, letters were sealed with wax. The wax was embossed with a design by pressing a carved gemstone into it before it hardened. These stones were carved with countless images—butterflies, alone and in combination with other devices, among them. The Emperor Augustus chose as his emblem a butterfly held in the claws of a crab, accompanied by the motto "*festina lente*" (make haste slowly). A woodcut of the emblem appears in Geoffrey Whitney's *Choice of Emblems,* first published in 1586 (plate 54).

A butterfly, because it is so fragile, seems to be an unlikely symbol for any of the heroic qualities usually associated with the bearing of arms. However, there is at least one case in which a family reversed the usual order by shower-

49

ing prestige upon the arms it bore, which consisted of three butterflies in a field. The Papillons were a family of Huguenots whose members held positions of trust and responsibility in the courts of the kings of France for over three hundred years. The term "iron butterfly," which, in the twentieth century, is applied to a woman of frail appearance but strong will, could have been applied equally well to the Papillons, who refused to relinquish their faith despite the atrocities and persecutions suffered by their sect and by their kin. One member lost his life in the Saint Bartholomew's Day massacre, two were victims of the guillotine during the French Revolution, and one was exiled. Some fled from France after the massacre, and others after the revocation of the Edict of Nantes, but there are members of the family still living today in both England and France. A fascinating sidelight to these migrations is the appearance in Montpelier, Vermont, of a family by the name of Butterfly. Most of the men had married French Canadian wives, and one man was actually named Napoleon Butterfly. Undoubtedly, they were originally Papillons who Anglicized their name after emigrating to the New World—a common practice at that time.

Butterflies probably first appeared on the shield of Papillon de Champagne before the end of the fifteenth century. The blazon is "vert with three butterflies or." At least seven members of the family bore arms in which butterflies were displayed, the last grant in France being made at the end of the eighteenth century at Chalon. In heraldic language it is described: "azure a chevron argent in chief two butterflies and in point a coq all or." In England, arms containing butterflies were granted in 1903 to the thirteenth lineal descendant of Antoine Papillon, a member of the court of Francis I and friend of Erasmus.

In other cases it is not possible to discover why butterflies were chosen as family emblems. For instance, the first arms containing a butterfly ever granted by the College of Heralds in London was to a family of musicians by the name of Bassano (plates 55, 56). The original Bassano, Antonio, emigrated to England from Italy about 1537. He and his extensive family served as court musicians to Henry VIII, Mary I, Elizabeth I, James I, and Charles I. Which member received the grant of arms cannot be proved. A butterfly, since it lacks the capacity for making any audible sound whatever, is indeed a strange emblem for a musical family. Many insects could have symbolized the musical profession quite well—crickets, locusts, click beetles, and bees are all makers of music. But the butterfly comes silently into the world and as silently leaves it without ever having made any sound at all. The one known exception is a genus of South American butterflies which the Bassanos, in all probability, never heard of. Nevertheless, according to the blazon, the arms granted to Bassano have a laurel branch in base, three butterflies in chief, and another butterfly as a crest. The only clue to their meaning is in a description of the arms which appeared in Glover's *History of Derbyshire* nearly two hundred years later. In this work, the butterflies are both described and pictured as *moths*, and the laurel branch of the original blazon is called a mulberry tree. There seems to be only one possible explanation. In 1633, when the arms are thought

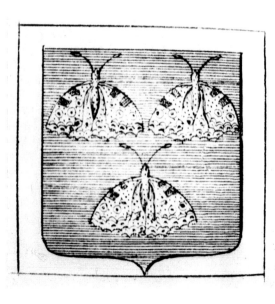

to have been granted, Italy was the hub of the silk industry. It is known that the Bassanos were in close touch with their Italian relations. If one of the Bassanos had been responsible for providing the royal family with unusually fine silken goods, he might have been rewarded with a grant of arms; if so, he could have chosen a silk moth as the emblem of his good fortune.

Still more cryptic is the coat of arms of Barin du Bois Geffroy et de la Galissonnière (plates 57, 58). Individual members of this noted French family at one time or another included a Lieutenant of the Naval Forces of France, and a member of the Naval Academy at Brest. One member took part in the siege of Candie, and another was decorated with the Grand Croix Honoraire de Saint-Louis. It is difficult to imagine a less suitable emblem than a butterfly for such men as these! There is no clue to the origin of the arms of Barin, which is blazoned "*azure à trois papillons or.*" For the present at least, its meaning must remain one of the mysteries of butterfly symbolism.

What the trappings of heraldry were to nobles and knights of the Middle Ages, the *mon* was to the Japanese prince, or Daimyo. Most Daimyos had three *mons*. The most important, the *jō-mon,* invariably appeared five times on ceremonial garments. It was also displayed on the prince's possessions—his palanquin, sword, armor, war banner, saddle cloth, lanterns, and the clothing of his servants. The second *mon,* called *kai-mon,* was embroidered or woven into ordinary clothing. It sometimes appeared on small roof tiles, while *jō-mon* was placed prominently over the doorway.

Daimyo Matsudaria of the province of Inaba, Lord of the Resting Butterflies, had butterflies at rest on his second and third *mon.* All three *mons* of Daimyo Ikeda of the province of Bizen were butterflies. In the eighteenth century, actors of the Kabuki theater were identified by their *mons*. At least six of them wore butterfly *mons,* among them Sanjo Kantaro, famous for the finesse with which he interpreted female roles (plate 59).

The butterfly signature that the artist James A.M. Whistler developed over the years and the butterfly-bedecked Volkswagen of the late rock star Janis Joplin served equally well to identify their owners. And on the opposite side of the world, the chosen name of Queen Rosaherina of Madagascar was "The Chrysalis" because she believed that her body was but a protecting case from which her soul would burst forth at death, as a butterfly breaks from its chrysalis.

In the murals at Tepantitla, Mexico, a scene occurs which is oddly reminiscent of the fowling scenes of ancient Egypt. This scene is thought to represent either an earthly paradise or the house of the rain god Tlaloc, in which the souls of the dead gather. The upper part of the painting is devoted to Tlaloc, who has a spider hanging above his head symbolizing the bond between heaven and earth. The lower panel is filled with droll little people engaged in all sorts of carefree pursuits. Some are dancing, singing, or playing games, but most are wielding nets and chasing huge butterflies. As in ancient Egypt, butterflies appear to have been one of the pleasures to be hoped for in the afterworld.

There is fragmentary evidence that the Egyptians regarded the butterfly

59. *above:* A Japanese mirror of solid copper bearing a familiar butterfly design which also occurs on the *mon* of the Tani family, on the costume of Sanjo Kantaro, and on the second *mon* of Daimyo Matsudaria Inaba no Kami, Lord of the Resting Butterflies. Date not known; probably modern. Collection Mrs. Martin Kamar.

60. *left:* Clay incensario cover, Pre-Columbian (Teotjhuacan III). American Museum of Natural History, New York. The kinship between butterflies and fire is well illustrated in this handsome decorative lid, which depicts Xochipilli, the god of spring, with a butterfly at his lips. Other butterflies are seen flying into the flames which surmount the entire structure.

emerging from its chrysalis as symbolic of the soul of the dead leaving the body, but certainly for them it was not a major concept. The opposite is true of the Pre-Columbian tribal societies. Probably nowhere else in the world has butterfly symbolism played as important a role as it did in the religious beliefs of the Mexican and Central American Indian cultures.

Butterflies were closely related to other symbols of heat, light, and regeneration, which together signified life. Heat had its origin deep in the womb of the earth, whence it periodically burst forth with a great roar. Itzpapolotl (The Obsidian Butterfly), a goddess of the earth and stars, owed her name to the lustrous black glass which results from volcanic eruption. During sacrificial rites concerning the fire god, a human being was burned alive, the flames symbolizing rebirth. In paintings, butterflies are sometimes shown as little flying flames with round heads. In Teotihuacan, incensarios used in sacrificial rites had elaborately beautiful covers ornamented with symbols of life and renewal, including many butterflies; these were enveloped in smoke when fires were lit beneath them (plate 60).

Light was exemplified by the sun, of which the butterfly was a symbol. Numerous gods and goddesses were responsible for the renewal of life. The butterfly was the symbol of the many-faceted earth goddess, Xochiquetzal, mother of gods and men and consort of the fire god. She followed young men into battle and cohabited with them, and wore a butterfly at her lips, as did Xochipilli, the god of flowers and the greening of the year. Regeneration through human sacrifice was the subject of many rites. That in honor of Xipe Toltec, the flayed god and the god of seed time, was one of the most dreadful. The victim was skinned alive, and upon his death a priest donned his flayed skin as a symbol of the renewal of the earth's vegetation. Xipe too was depicted with a butterfly at his lips.

There is an overriding sense of violence about the butterfly symbolism of the Pre-Columbians, which does not occur elsewhere. Butterfly pectorals are worn by the warriors in stone which dominate the temples at Tula and Chichén Itzá, and by the warriors at Tenochtitlán. The great god-king, Quetzalcoatl, also wore a butterfly pectoral. He was the first to abolish human sacrifice and offered instead certain animals which had divine significance, including snakes and butterflies.

The Pre-Columbian approach to mysticism was in sharp contrast to that of the ancient Chinese. Reverence for life, an integral part of the Buddhist faith, extends not only to butterflies but to all insects. The legendary Buddhist priest, Jizo, is pictured carrying a staff ornamented with musical rings which jingle as he moves; its purpose is to alert any insects upon which he might otherwise tread.

An early Taoist philosopher, Chuang Tzu, believed that he lay dormant during the daytime, but that at night he awoke transformed into a butterfly and flew about sipping nectar in a flower garden. As he thought about this, he found he could not decide whether he was really a butterfly or a man. It might be, he reasoned, that he was a man during the night dreaming that he was a butterfly by day. This identity crisis resulted in a lengthy philosophical argument which still has its repercussions. Perhaps Chuang Tzu secretly thought the carefree life of a butterfly so desirable that in his subconscious mind he was, indeed, a butterfly. In any case, he certainly did not subscribe to the Western idea that man was given dominion over the earth and all other animals. He took the Buddhist view that man was but a part of the spectrum of life, and that, although superior to other animals, he could learn much by observing and studying them. Western man can, without qualms, catch and kill a butterfly. A Chinese would rather contemplate it—a more popular view among naturalists than scientists.

# Metamorphosis

*Sing Cocoon*

The little caterpillar creeps
Awhile before in silk it sleeps.
It sleeps awhile before it flies,
And flies awhile before it dies,
And that's the end of three good tries.

DAVID MCCORD

The word "metamorphosis" is derived from two Greek words and means "many changes." As applied to insects, it means the transformations which take place in their bodies before they reach the adult stage. Lepidoptera undergo *complete* metamorphosis. In other words, their life cycle consists of four stages, each entirely different from the other three. The first of these, the embryonic stage, is carried out in a minuscule egg. In the case of very small butterflies, such as the hairstreaks and checkerspots, a hundred eggs would not occupy a space three-sixteenths of an inch square. Larger butterflies, such as the swallowtails, have larger eggs, not more than four of which would rest comfortably on the head of a pin (plate 61). When laid, the eggs are very light in color—pale green, creamy yellow, or white. They darken, and finally become black before hatching.

The second, or larval stage, when the insect is a caterpillar, is divided into five instars, each punctuated by the shedding of a larval skin. The appearance of the caterpillar often changes with each moult. When these five instars have been completed, some caterpillars change color completely before pupating. The tiger swallowtail (*Papilio glaucus*), for instance, turns from bright green to chocolate brown, and the spicebush swallowtail (*P. troilus*), from leaf green to butter yellow.

Thus before reaching the pupal stage (the third stage in the metamorphosis of the butterfly), a caterpillar may already have presented ten visible aspects.

Indeed, the life of a butterfly, viewed in its entirety for the first time, seems less possible than do those fantastic creatures indigenous to the medieval mind which are found only in the bestiaries. There seems to be no logic in a butterfly. Its life begins in an egg which is fertilized a fraction of a second before it is laid on a leaf or a blade of grass. About five days later, the future butterfly crawls forth in the form of a caterpillar less than one millimeter in length, often invisible to the naked untrained eye. When newly hatched, the larvae are apt to be putty-colored with glistening black heads. They can melt to invisibility in the smallest crease—the faintest shadow of the leaf, into which they eat only pinholes in this, their first instar.

In a day or two, the caterpillar's skin becomes smooth and taut, finally splits, and the little creature again crawls forth. By this time the special characteristics of each caterpillar are more evident. With a magnifying glass, it is possible to tell one species from another.

Of its sixteen legs, it uses only the last ten for crawling. It moves in waves, lifting one pair of soft little stubs after the other, from the first to the last. By contrast, the six front legs are stiff and sharply pointed, and although they may touch the leaf, they do not cling to it. As it crawls, the caterpillar spins a continuous thread of silk which is even less visible than the caterpillar itself. As it grows, its appearance becomes even more fantastic. In some species the skin takes on irregular blotches. Some develop long spines, large round spots, multicolored stripes or bands. Some assume cryptic postures. Others are able to extrude forked glands which give off an evil odor. Caterpillars of moths can be even more grotesque than those of butterflies, exhibiting horns, clusters of stinging bristles, long threadlike tails, or thick coats of fur. By the end of the fifth and final instar, there is no limit to the weird appendages and designs with which caterpillars are decorated (plates 62–65).

At the end of two weeks, having increased its original bulk as much as 30,000 times, the caterpillar crawls to some secluded place, spins a support with the last of its silk, sheds its final skin, and immediately assumes a new form—legless, headless, and immobilized. This is the third stage of its metamorphosis. It has become a chrysalis. A shell hardens around it, and it remains mummy-like, apparently lifeless. About ten days pass, and then the colors of wings can be seen through the shell. A day or two later the chrysalis opens, and the perfect butterfly appears.

How baffling is the sequence in which there are apparently two embryonic stages, resulting in two entirely different creatures. From an egg has come a caterpillar; from a chrysalis a butterfly. Even Aristotle, a scholar of extraordinary versatility, was not able to solve the mystery entirely, for he wrote: ". . . by the union of the sexes something is produced, not the same in any

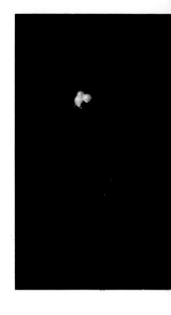

61. The eggs of the black swallowtail, *Papilio polyxenes asterius,* are laid on parsley, carrot and other plants of the family Umbelliferae. To show their size three eggs have been placed on head of a pin.

62. *left:* Brassolidae, Malaya. Butterfly larva. It is astonishing to see the extremes to which caterpillars have evolved to protect themselves. It is possible that some Lepidoptera may be poisonous or distasteful in the larval stage but palatable as butterflies. It is also possible that harmless larvae may mimic distasteful larvae. In any case, this one from Malaya is cryptically marked, while those from Brazil (plate 63) and Thailand (plate 64) are aposematic.

63. *right:* Nymphalidae, Brazil. Butterfly larva.

64. *below:* Lepidopterous larva, Thailand.

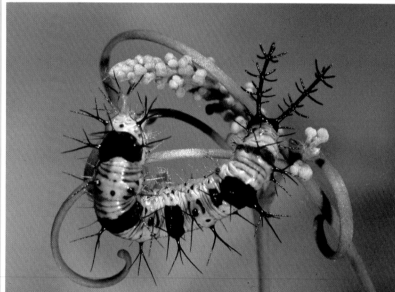

65. *right:* Heliconiidae: *Marpesia petreus,* United States. This caterpillar of the butterfly called the ruddy dagger wing is disruptively colored. Under ordinary circumstances it would probably be sufficiently disguised by its markings and camouflaged in its surroundings to escape attention. This individual was apparently seen by a bird while in the act of spinning. The long spines may have deterred the predator, or the copious silk may have prevented it from snatching the caterpillar entirely free of its weaving. At any rate, the bird departed, leaving the caterpillar suspended in midair.

respect, but an imperfect animal—as from butterflies are produced egg-like worms, from which neither similar creatures are produced, nor any other creature, but such things only. . . . Most [insects] produce their young very soon after sexual intercourse. All kinds except some psychae produce worms. These produce a hard substance like the seed of the cnecus, which is fluid within. From the worm an animal is produced, but not a portion of it, as if it were an ovum, but the whole grows and becomes an articulated animal. . . . Butterflies are produced from caterpillars, and these originate in the leaves of green plants.''

Little by little, enquiring minds and ever more sophisticated techniques of modern science have been solving the mystery of the butterfly. We can now understand some of the marvelous invisible changes which cause the changes we can see. We know, for instance, that the little egg, hardly larger than a pinprick, contains all the genetic material and the capacity for producing all the hormones, ectases, and glandular secretions necessary for the precise and complicated process which will eventually produce a butterfly. We know that this egg, at first a microscopic speck of protoplasm, is incipient even in the body of a newly hatched caterpillar.

By the time the female butterfly emerges, all of her eggs, usually three to four hundred, are stored in cobweb-thin tubes in her abdomen. Also in her abdomen is a sac known as the bursa copulatrix, and into this sac, when she mates, the male butterfly deposits a much smaller sac, containing enough sperm to fertilize all the eggs she will lay. The eggs grow as they travel down the tubes in which they were formed, but, each egg being a single unfertilized cell, they do not multiply. The sperm makes its long and tortuous passage from the bursa through a different tube, but the journeys of both egg and sperm

66. *opposite left:* Lycaenidae: *Arawacus lincoides,*
Brazil. The male butterfly approaches the female
during courtship, prior to mating.

67. *right:* Pieridae: *Melete lycimnia,* Venezuela.
Butterflies in copula.

68. *below:* Nymphalidae: *Phyciodes tharos,* United
States. Butterflies in copula. When mating, the male
grasps the abdomen of the female between claspers at
the end of his own abdomen. Thus if threatened he is
able to fly, carrying her with him.

end at a common point near the tip of the butterfly's abdomen, and, as the egg passes the tube containing the sperm, it is fertilized.

The butterfly lifts her wings and, grasping the edge of a leaf with clawed feet, curves her abdomen downward to meet it. The eggs are thus laid, sometimes singly, sometimes in clusters, sometimes all at once, but by each butterfly on the special plant which her own offspring can eat, for each caterpillar is nourished by a particular kind of food without which it would perish.

We have discovered that, as soon as the egg is laid, cells begin to divide and multiply. At first, a ring of new cells forms just inside the shell, which causes the color of the egg to darken. When the caterpillar is fully formed, its head lies at the top of the egg and can be seen, black and glistening, through the transparent shell.

The caterpillar hatches and grows, but the butterfly's special organs are prevented from maturing by a hormone excreted from a pair of glands near the caterpillar's head, known as the corpora allata. Thus, the cell clusters which will form the butterfly's reproductive organs, compound eyes, antennae, and wings remain dormant until the caterpillar is fully grown.

The caterpillar grows larger and therefore more visible. To compensate, it must, at the same time, become either less visible to its natural enemies through camouflage or more frightening by assuming some fantastic disguise. It is clear that both means of protection have evolved with marked success, since butterflies have existed on earth for more than fifty million years. Caterpillars face many hazards. They are food for mice, moles, toads, birds, and other small animals, as well as for other insects, and especially for spiders. We now understand that the function of the disruptive blotches and the colorful stripes, which blend into sunlit foliage, is to aid the caterpillar in concealing itself. Likewise, gradually shaded colors (formed by microscopic white dots) and pencil-thin dark lines on a cylindrical body make it appear flat when seen against a leaf.

Multicolored encircling bands are also effective warning devices, for some caterpillars so clothed are poisonous to birds and mammals. These are imitated by other caterpillars, which in turn gain some slight advantage. Some caterpillars are disguised as snakes by realistic eyespots and green skin, forked scent glands, and the habit of resting in a rolled leaf with only the thorax showing. This mimicry is a powerful deterrent to birds, which often panic at the sight of a snake. The spines, flowing tails, humps, bristles, and horns are all part of an elaborate parade of deception—a series of life-saving tools by which a slow and cumbersome creature may be saved from death many times during a day. However eerie or clownish, however revolting or frightening or monstrous a caterpillar may seem, its appearance is a protection from its own particular enemies in its own specific environment. Otherwise it would not be alive.

When the caterpillar is fully grown, there comes a period when it is no longer a caterpillar and not yet a chrysalis. This stage is called the prepupal stadium. It begins when the caterpillar stops feeding and ends when the chrysalis shell has hardened—a period of perhaps sixty hours. It is a time of resting, of changing color, of excreting wastes and shrinking in size. It is a time of crawling blindly into unfamiliar territory, sometimes for only a few feet, some-

69. *above:* A caterpillar in the second instar, ready to moult, and a full-grown caterpillar. In the early stages the caterpillar of this swallowtail is protected from its natural enemies by its resemblance to a bird dropping.

*Opposite:*
70. *above left:* Papilionidae: *Papilio polyxenes,* United States. Caterpillars of this family have extrusible glands behind the head which exude a musky odor repellent to birds.

71. *above right:* Limacodidae: *Euclea delphinii,* United States. There are stinging hairs in the ends of the spines of this handsome moth caterpillar. Some members of this family exude poisons not only painful but dangerous to human beings, and the sting of at least one species is fatal. But the brilliant colors and fantastic appearance serve as a warning to man and beast.

72. *right:* Ceratocampidae: *Citheronia regalis,* United States. Known as the hickory horndevil, this caterpillar later becomes the beautiful royal walnut moth. Its food plants include butternut and persimmon as well as walnut.

times for half a mile. It includes the last spinning of silk, the last shedding of skin (plates 73, 74). It ends after the hazardous hours when, hanging by silken threads from some new-found surface, lacking all of its former protections and not yet possessed of new ones, it is at the mercy of all its predators. At the onset of the prepupal stadium a feedback mechanism goes into effect, ending the production of the juvenile hormone which has been constantly flowing in minute quantities from the corpora allata. This presages the end of larval life. The cell clusters of the butterfly begin to multiply, and vast changes take place within the caterpillar, for its organs break down as the organs of the butterfly grow. All this is accomplished with the aid of particles in the blood called phagocytes, similar to leucocytes in human blood. These phagocytes feed on the degenerating organs of the caterpillar, while the growing cells of the butterfly feed on the waste products of the phagocytes. By this process, the marvelous transition from creeping earthbound larva to free spirit of the air has begun. Chewing mandibles, spinning gland, massive digestive organs, crawling feet will gradually disappear, as proboscis, antennae, reproductive system, jointed legs, and above all the magnificent wings begin to grow. The simple ocelli, eyes of pinprick size through which the caterpillar could do little more than distinguish light from darkness, are transformed into magnificent compound orbs, each containing 36,000 units of sight. A new skin forms beneath the caterpillar's old skin. On the thorax (the area between the head and the abdomen), the wing cells begin to multipy, and the wings to form inside the caterpillar's body. At the same time the butterfly's antennae and proboscis begin to take shape. Finally the old skin is shed, and the tenuous beginnings

73. *above far left:* During the prepupal stadium the caterpillar uses the last of its silk to spin a supporting belt.

74. *above left:* After resting whil inner changes take place, the caterpillar sheds its last larval sk and becomes a chrysalis. The beginnings of the butterfly's eyes antennae, and wings can be seen briefly at this time.

75. *above:* A hard shell forms ov the pupa, and a two-week-long chrysalis stage begins.

of the new organs may be clearly seen. Thin triangular fore wings cover more rounded triangles of hind wings, all folded down across the abdomen. Legs, proboscis, and antennae lie in delicate threads between them. Pale globes on either side of the head mark the beginnings of compound eyes. Twenty-four hours later, the chrysalis shell will have hardened, and only dim outlines will mark where these miraculous changes were transiently visible (plate 75).

The chrysalis remains for two weeks, disguised as a broken twig, a bud, a leaf node—whatever can conceal it best. Finally the shell cracks (plate 76). A month earlier this creature had crawled from its egg shell. Four times subsequently it had crawled from its skin. Now its crawling is ended forever, and miraculously, it seems, a new creature has been born. The butterfly pushes its way into the world, clings to some nearby surface while its wrinkled little wings expand and harden. Then suddenly it explodes into the air—a tiny spark in the great procession of life, yet a masterpiece of color, radiance, and design, unsurpassed in the whole panorama of creation.

76. *above:* At the end of the second week, the shell cracks along the ventral side, and a butterfly crawls forth.

77. *right:* An hour after it has emerged, its wings fully extended and veins hardened now, the butterfly rests on a flower petal after its first short flight.

78. Heliconiidae. Possibly *Heliconius melpomene* or *Heliconius erato*.

# Wings

## THE FORMATION OF WINGS

There are several theories as to how insect wings originated. Perhaps the most acceptable is that some prehistoric leaping insect (such as a distant ancestor of the grasshopper) developed little folds of skin on its thorax. These folds helped it to sail and to steer itself as it leapt from one perch toward another. Over the millennia, these membranous folds became larger and stronger, while the jumping legs grew less and less essential, and as a result less powerful, until eventually the function of the legs was merely to help the insect to leave the ground, while the membranous wing-folds, having become capable of longer and longer guided forays into the air, were the real agents of locomotion. From some such small beginnings, more than a hundred million years ago, the superbly efficient and specialized wings of our butterflies and moths evolved.

Not only are the wings efficient, so is the process by which they are formed: starting as little clusters of undifferentiated cells, they are shaped, structured, and everted in about three days.

The breakdown and buildup of the digestive and reproductive organs

65

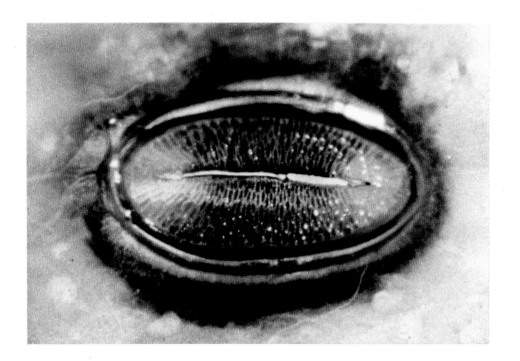

79. Sphingidae. A greatly magnified spiracle of a Mexican sphinx-moth larva.

which takes place during metamorphosis has already been briefly described. The muscular system also changes radically, for while crawling muscles are no longer a necessity for the butterfly, flying muscles must be developed. Only the circulatory and respiratory systems remain more or less intact. It is necessary to know a little bit about these systems in order to understand some of the mysteries of a butterfly's wings.

    Insects differ from mammals in that they have no veins and arteries and no lungs. In mammals, the blood flows unceasingly through a complicated network of blood vessels, and air exchange takes place when it reaches the lungs. The emerald-green blood of a butterfly is circulated through a single long tube by a series of muscular pumps within it. This tube runs along the length of the butterfly's back. The blood is pulled into it from the end of the abdomen and is sprayed out into its head, whence it flows freely throughout the body over all the organs.

80. The formation of butterfly wings. Diagrams by Jean Hus

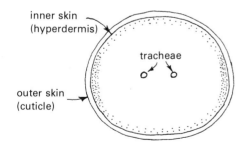

Undifferentiated cells of the hyperdermis are ready to form the wings.

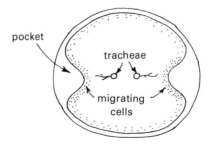

Cells begin to differentiate and migrate inward to form pocket.

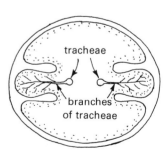

Reversing direction, cells move toward outer skin, filling pocket and forming wings. Branches of tracheae penetrate spaces between two layers of wing cells.

In place of lungs, the caterpillar, and later the butterfly, has a series of small openings on the sides of its body called spiracles through which it breathes. The spiracles are the outward openings of tracheae, tubes which branch into hundreds of minute tubelets called tracheoles. These tracheoles reach into all the recesses of the body. Air travels into the spiracles, through the tracheae, and into all of their branches. Air exchange is effected through the tracheoles.

The tracheae, and the inner layer of the caterpillar's skin (called the hyperdermis), are the two essential elements from which the wings of the butterfly are formed. The dormant wing cells are part of the inner skin of the caterpillar. They are located in the last two segments of the thorax, one pair on each segment (plate 80, no. 1). When the caterpillar is fully grown, the juvenile hormone ceases to flow, and these cells begin to multiply, pushing inward. In this way they form a small pocket between the inner and the outer skin (plate 80, no. 2). Having formed this pocket, they then reverse their direction, and more cells, growing outward but still inside the caterpillar's body, form a little budlike swelling (plate 80, no. 3). The two sides of this bud will become the upper and lower membranes of the wing. At this point they are thick and puffy and separated from each other. As the wing continues to develop, one of the tracheae, or breathing tubes, located in the thorax sends out a branch which penetrates into the wing bud between the two layers of the membrane. This branch will divide further and eventually form the veins of the wing. Other cells form minute filaments which become attached to both membranes, holding them together. The cells continue to multiply and differentiate, and the wing grows. After the caterpillar has attached itself to a support, but before it pupates, the wing pushes out of the pocket where it was formed. It now lies against the outside of the body, but underneath the old skin, which is already beginning to loosen in preparation for being shed (plate 80, no. 4). In some species, these little wing buds can be detected just before the old skin is shed.

Only after this final ecdysis is the new wing fully exposed (plate 80, no. 5). It begins immediately to stretch out. As it grows longer, the minute strands holding one side to the other tighten, pulling the two membranes closer to-

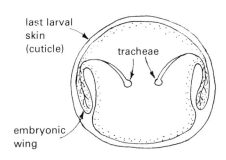

Embryonic wings evert and lie in pockets against outside of body wall, but inside of last larval skin.

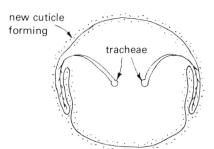

Last larval skin has been shed. The forming wings are visible for the first time. New cuticle starts to form.

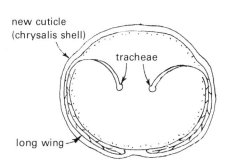

New cuticle made by excretions of endocrine glands hardens and protects the forming butterfly. In 24 hours wings have radically changed in size and shape.

gether and drawing them into a series of microscopic pleats. Simultaneously a new shell begins to harden over the chrysalis, and the new wings are secured beneath it. Already they are more than eight times as large as they were at the moment when the skin was shed (plate 80, no. 6).

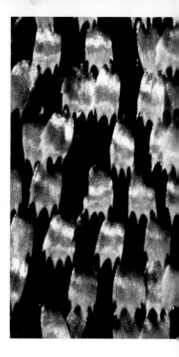

## WING SCALES

What makes the butterfly so strikingly different from all other insects is that its wings are covered with colored scales. The interplay between the wings of butterflies and the sunlight makes them easy rivals of the most exotic flowers and the most exquisite gemstones, with which they have often been compared. It is really these colored scales (combined with the great size of the wings) which have generated in man an irresistible fascination. Where did these scales come from? How are they made into patterns? What are they for? Nothing is more amazing than the answers to these questions. Nothing is more amazing than the extravagant array of genetic material which is stored to make the mosaic of a butterfly's wings, and the precision with which it is loosed.

The wing scales of butterflies, like the scales of fish and the feathers of birds, are modified hairs, which may originally have acted only as a protection for the wing surfaces. Strange as it may seem, a butterfly's scales do serve to strengthen the wing to a certain extent, since they are minutely ridged, which gives them firmness, and since they overlap each other, forming a protective mantle for the wing membranes. It is possible that hundreds of millions of years ago this was the only function of the scales that they were all dull of color, hairlike of shape, and scattered more or less randomly over the surfaces of the wings. If this is the case, there are some moths which today still retain the same primitive characteristics. If this is the case, the glittering scales of our present-day butterflies are the product of a refinement which has been in process since the first insect grew wings, and one may say with confidence that nowhere in the animal kingdom is the process of evolution more dramatically demonstrated.

At first the wing consists of two simple transparent membranes with the forming veins sandwiched between them. But there are certain specialized wing cells endowed with the function of manufacturing scales. These cells deposit a row of scales on the ridge of each newly made wing pleat. At first the scales are little bubbles of green blood lying along the ridges of the wing like a layer of foam. Each separate scale is attached to the membrane by a minuscule ball-and-socket type of hinge. As they develop, they stretch and flatten. Soon they begin to differentiate, each according to the function it will ultimately perform. This process of transfiguration continues inside the chrysalis until the butterfly is ready to emerge. A few hours before this time arrives, the colors and patterns of the fore wings can be seen in miniature through the translucent chrysalis shell.

81. *top:* Papilionidae: *Troides victoriae rubianus,* Guadalcanal. Toothed scales having a pearly iridescence hide darker pigment scales beneath. Underneath side wings of a female.

82. *center:* Papilionidae: *Papilio ulysses,* New Guinea. Like the Morphos of Brazil, this lovely butterfly from the South Seas shines with a shimmering blue iridescence which has never been duplicated in any man-made object.

# OF WINGS LIKE COLORED GLASS

Of all the butterflies in the world, none are more spectacular than those of the family Papilionidae, usually called the swallowtails, although many are, in fact, tail-less.

The largest of all butterflies, the birdwings, belong to this family. Opinions differ as to how these spectacular insects should be classified, but those which appear in this book fall into four general groups. These are: the *priamus* group (genus *Ornithoptera*), which are geographic varietal forms of the same species; *Troides,* including species and forms of the Victoria and Alexandra birdwings, the female of the latter being the largest butterfly in the world; *Trogonoptera,* including Rajah Brooke's birdwing (*brookiana* and its related forms); and *Papilio paradisea*, which is one of the only two species of tailed birdwings.

Most North American swallowtails, beautiful as they are, lack the iridescence of many tropical species, excepting on the hind-wing borders, which are wider beneath than above.

The Morphos (family Morphidae) of the American tropics rival the birdwings in magnificence but not in the variety of their colors. The wings of the male Morphos glow with shimmering blue or pearly white, while those of the birdwings cover a spectrum ranging from orange-gold to deep purple with wine-pink fractions.

83. *above right:* Papilionidae:
*Papilio ulysses,* Australia.
Iridescent blue scales and gray-black hair scales are juxtaposed to form the fascinating three-dimensional pattern. It occurs on the fore wings of the males of this species but not of the females.

84. *right:* Papilionidae:
*Ornithoptera priamus croesus,*
Philippines. Gold areas of the female's hind wings are bordered with pale-green reflecting scales.

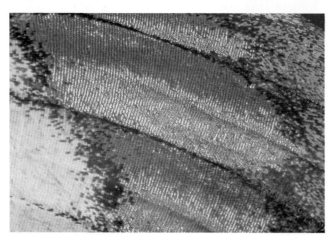

85. *left:* Pieridae: *Colotis regina,* East Africa. This iridescent lavender patch is part of the wing tip of an otherwise white butterfly. Many African Pierids have colorful wing tips, those of the females often being quite different in color from the males.

86. *below:* Morphidae: *Morpho menelaus,* Peru. Basking in the sun.

87. *bottom left:* Morphidae: *Morpho rhetenor,* Peru. The iridescent blue of this and many other Morpho species is caused by the microscopic ridges of light-refracting scales. The color is therefore dependent on the angle of refraction as the sun's light glances off the wing's surface. Here the iridescence is visible, in plate 88 it is not.

88. *bottom right:* Morphidae: *Morpho rhetenor,* Peru.

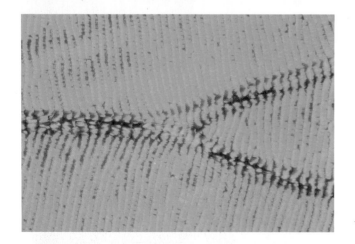

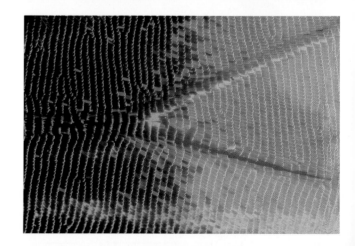

89. *far left:* Papilionidae: *Thais polyxena,* Bulgaria. This distinctive genus cannot be confused with any other.

90. *left:* Papilionidae: *Thais rumina,* Spain.

91. *above:* Papilionidae: *Papilio paradisea,* New Guinea. A male *paradisea,* one of the rarest and most exotic of butterflies. The females are quite different from the males, being black and white and lacking the distinctive hind-wing tails.

92. *right:* Papilionidae: *Papilio paradisea,* New Guinea. This design appears on the underside of the hind wings of the male.

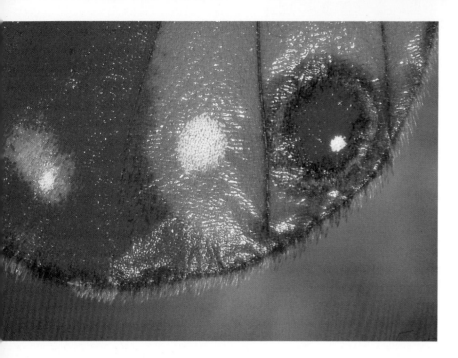

93. *left:* Satyridae: *Cithaerias pyropina,* Peru.

94. *below:* Satyridae: *Pierella hyalinus,* Trinidad. Unlike most members of its family, which are brown and rather drab, this lovely Satyrid seems more like a swallowtail in both color and shape. It inhabits the jungle, where it may seen near rotting fruit or vegetation, which it prefers to nectar.

95. *opposite:* Papilionidae: *Parnassius clodius,* United States. The Parnassians have an interesting habit. While in copula, males deposit a structure known as a sphragis on the abdomen of the female; this apparently prevents her from mating a second time. In each species the structure is slightly different. Since the Parnassians tend to vary considerably in color and pattern, the sphragis, which can be clearly seen in this picture, is a valuable characteristic in identification of the species.

When Shakespeare wrote in *Troilus and Cressida*

. . . for men like butterflies
Show not their mealy wings but to the summer

he was referring to the fine powdery "meal" which is left on the fingers when one gently rubs the wing of a butterfly. The scales do indeed seem like powder to the naked eye, but through a microscope they are discovered to be of many shapes and textures, minutely structured, splendidly colored—each a micro-jewel, each making its own particular contribution to the life of the butterfly.

The colors of the wing scales are of two varieties. Some scales are colored by pigment which is manufactured in the insect's body during metamorphosis. Other colors are structural. These are made by microscopic striations on certain special scales. Such scales act as prisms, refracting the sunlight and producing an array of glittering psychedelic hues. The cerulean wings of the Brazilian Morphos, the green fire of the great birdwing butterflies of New Guinea and Sumatra, the rainbow hues of the swallowtails of Sikkim, and the glittering wing surfaces of many smaller butterflies are all caused by the refraction of light.

In a general way, it may be said that yellow, white, brown, black, and red are made from pigment, while blues, greens, gold, and silver are structural.

74

16. *opposite:* Nymphalidae: *Vanessa atalanta,* United States. This butterfly, widespread both here and in Europe, appears symbolically in the art of the late Middle Ages and that of the Renaissance. One reason for its use in this connection was the "devil's face" that appears on the underside of its hind wings. In this spread specimen both faces are clearly visible.

17. *right:* Papilionidae: *Papilio troilus,* United States. At least four eastern swallowtails belong to a mimicry complex for which the pipe-vine swallowtail *(Battus philenor)* is the model. The mimics are *Papilio troilus* (spice-bush swallowtail), *Limenitis astayanax* (red-spotted purple), and the females of *Papilio polyxenes* (black swallowtail), *Speyeria diana* (diana fritillary), and *Papilio glaucus* (tiger swallowtail). The model feeds on Aristolochia, a poisonous plant, in the larval stages and is poisonous. The mimics are not.

But many light-reflecting scales are also pigmented. The regal aspect of England's purple emperor results from a combination of black pigment and striations reflecting blue light, the red of the copper butterflies from red pigment and clear light. It is the combination of these circumstances that makes possible the dazzling panorama of colors found in the wings of butterflies—an array covering the entire spectrum of visible light.

Even more remarkable is the process by which pigments are manufactured so that each individual butterfly can be recognized as a member of its particular species. This is not to say that the wings are the only criterion used in classifying a butterfly, for the palpi, legs, antennae, wing veins, and genitalia all play important roles in this complicated unraveling process. In fact, many insects must still be reared and their early stages scrutinized before they can be identified with certainty. But any true nature lover with the help of a good field guide can identify most of the species of butterflies in his area by their wings alone. This is because the patterns, shapes, and colors of the wings of each species can be predicted in each individual. Most have changed little

75

throughout the recorded history of mankind. Butterflies painted in the tomb of Beni Hassan in the twelfth dynasty can easily be identified as *Danaus chrysippus* by the pattern and color of the wings, if not the shape. Fossil butterflies found at Lake Florissant in Colorado can be partially classified by the veins, the shape, and even in some cases by the pattern of the wings (plate 98).

The scale pigments are made from chemicals within the insect's body and are transported by the blood, which, as has been said, flows freely through all parts of the insect's body, including the scales of the embryonic wings. Some device must obviously exist to control the growth of scales and the production and distribution of colors. Otherwise, the wings of all butterflies would be a dull and universal brown. The device is a complex system of biological time clocks and feedback mechanisms controlled by genes or hormones. Briefly it works as follows.

The forming scales do not all begin to grow at the same time, nor do they develop at the same rate of speed. Only when each separate scale has arrived at a certain stage of development will it be ready to accept the color that will be part of the unique pattern to which it belongs. Certain groups of scales reach the point of maturation at which they can accept color sooner than others.

The pigments are then released into the blood in such a manner that waves of color flow at certain moments. These moments are coordinated with

98. *Prodryas persephone.* Fossil specimen, found at the fossil bed of Lake Florissant, Colorado. Courtesy of Dr. F. M. Carpenter, Curator of Fossil Insects, Harvard University, Cambridge, Mass. This butterfly may be the only one of its kind ever seen by man. It lived seventy million years ago and became extinct before history was written. This specimen is thought to have died during the time of the Laramide Revolution, when volcanic ash fell on its wings, forcing it to the ground.

99. Acraeidae: *Acraea zambesina,* India. Veins on the underside of the hind wing. This butterfly is one of the few members of the Acraeidae family in India. There is only one species in Australia, but Africa has over forty. These butterflies are distasteful to birds and many, like the monarch, are orange or red and black. The center spot is at the edge of a closed wing cell.

the readiness of the proper scales to absorb them. Hence, when a particular color arrives in the wings, only the scales destined to bear that hue are ready to receive it. By flawless repetition of this process, the mosaic of the wings is laid in a matter of three days. It is a humbling experience to look through a microscope at a section of wing no larger than a modern contact lens and, looking, to contemplate the very fact of life itself—how it is capable of working out with such precision the formula for anything so beautiful as a butterfly.

## WING VEINS AND TEMPERATURE CONTROL

When the butterfly emerges from its chrysalis, blood is forced through the wing veins into its wings, causing them to expand. The minute wrinkles are smoothed out, and in about six minutes the butterfly has attained its full size. At first the veins are soft and pliable, and often translucent. In the black swallowtail (*Papilio polyxenes asterius*) and the other swallowtails belonging to the same group, they are pale yellow, and the green blood can be clearly seen through the large costal vein.

When the wings have completely expanded, the blood is recalled into the insect's body, and both membranes and veins begin to harden—a process which requires an hour or more. The butterfly is then ready for its first flight. The veins have become hollow tubes supporting the fabric of the membranes between which they are now laminated.

The wing veins are sometimes called nervures because, strictly speaking, they are not really veins. Their primary function is not the distribution of blood through the body, but strengthening the wings, thus making flight possible. Actually they are composed of two concentric tubes. The inner tube is filled with air. The outer tube retains a small amount of blood which, circulating slowly, provides lubrication and prevents the veins from becoming too brittle. It can also conduct a certain amount of heat back to the body. When butterflies alight on a rock and spread their wings after a cold or rainy night, it is to let these little rivers of blood in the wings be warmed by the sun. This is important since a butterfly has no built-in temperature control. The rate of flow of blood in its system fluctuates with the amount of heat in its surroundings, not in its body. A butterfly put into a refrigerator for an hour will appear dead, but returned to a patch of sun, it soon begins to revive as the heat again penetrates its wings.

Use of the sun for temperature control by butterflies is surprisingly sophisticated. It is present to some extent in all their activities. For instance, the little butterflies of the Arctic regions usually fly no higher than two feet from the ground, thus taking advantage of the heat radiating upward from the earth's surface after it has been warmed by the sun. By contrast, tropical butterflies, when not feeding in open meadows, often disappear into woods or seek the cool tops of trees.

Some Arctic butterflies bask on the ground, absorbing the sun's warmth through the dark scales of their open wings. While doing so, they face away from the sun, raising the head and thorax, thus creating an angle at which they are exposed to maximum radiation. In these species, the wings are darker and the vein walls thinner on the top surface than on the bottom. If a cloud passes over the sun, some species will immediately close their wings, sealing in the heat.

The sulphur butterflies of Alaska, Greenland, Labrador, and the Yukon Territory rest with closed wings, facing at right angles to the rays of the sun and leaning away from it. Centuries of evolutionary change have given these Arctic sulphurs a multitude of black scales on the underside of their hind wings, and through these the sun's heat reaches the wing veins, circulation is quickened, and warm blood is transported into the body. Such dark scaling does not occur on the hind wings of closely related temperate and tropical sulphurs, which have no urgent need to accumulate heat from the sun.

Arctic butterflies have few light-refracting scales, or none at all, while the great birdwing butterflies of the South Pacific and the Morphos of the South American tropics are sheathed with them. These scales, which give color not by absorbing but by reflecting light, probably aid tropical butterflies in maintaining a temperature of maximum efficiency by keeping some of the heat away from their bodies. In a great many species of butterflies, females are darker than males and consequently better equipped to absorb heat. The reasons for this are not yet entirely clear. In many instances, these females are mimics of other species, and many are protected by being less conspicuous than their mates. But perhaps also, the long flight made by the female as she lays her eggs and the actual process of egg laying may require more energy than the simple flight of the males.

Moths which are active only during the night cannot take advantage of the sun to supply bodily heat. Instead they employ an extremely rapid vibrating, or shivering, motion of the wing muscles, and by this concentrated exer-

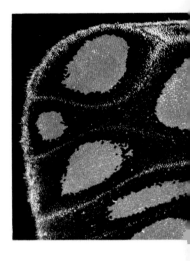

100. *above:* Zygaenidae, China. The moth family Zygaenidae is closely related to the Ctenuchidae. The main difference between the two is in the venation of the wings. Abundant in the Orient, the Zygaenidae spin silken cocoons.

101. *opposite:* Saturniidae: *Graellsia isabellae,* Spain. A section of the left fore wing. The family Saturniidae consists of three subfamilies, each distinguished from the others by minor differences in the venation of the hind wings. Wing veins are seldom as clearly visible as they are in this moth. Among butterflies, the familiar monarch is similarly marked. This moth is a threatened species in France.

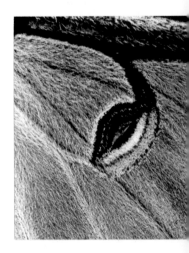

102. Saturniidae: *Actias luna,* United States. The costal margins of the wings of the luna moth are exceptionally strong. The decorative eyespots may be a protection against avian predators.

78

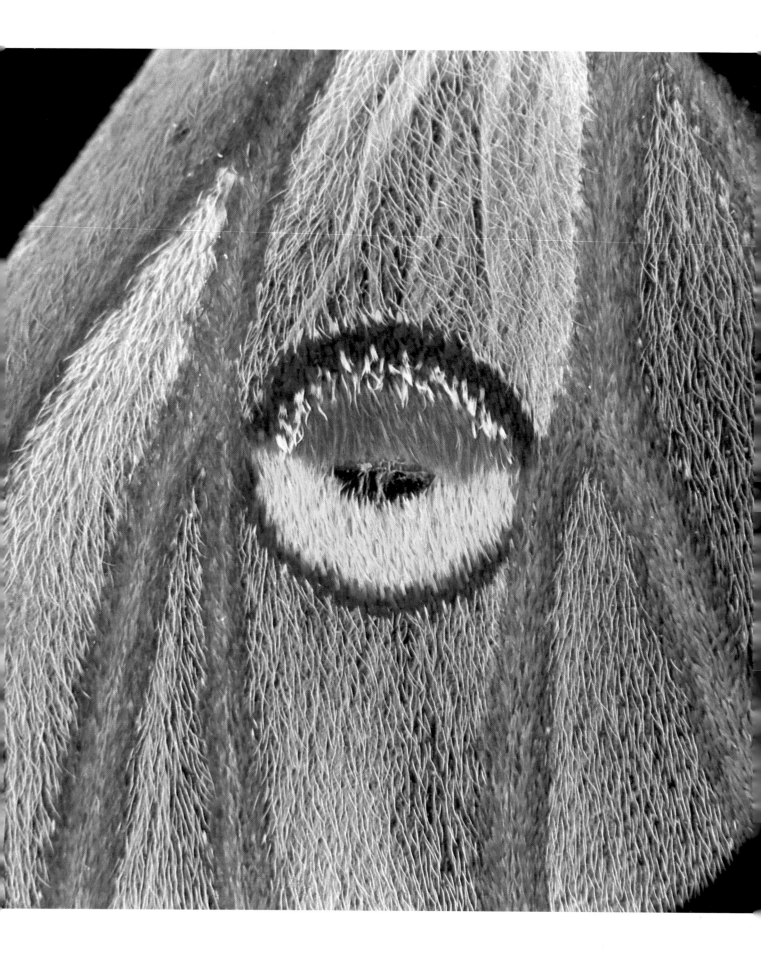

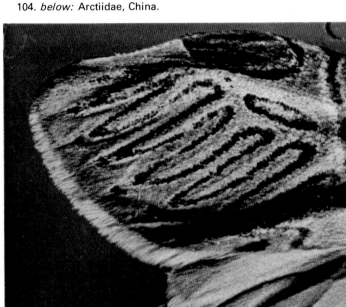

104. *below:* Arctiidae, China.

103. *above:* Arctiidae, French Guiana. Many features of the wings of the moth species here and in plate 104 are different, but the arrangement of the veins helps to identify them as belonging to the same family.

cise are able to generate approximately the same heat increase that butterflies acquire while basking quietly in the sun.

Wing veins are often clothed in black or near-black when the butterfly itself is of a lighter color, enabling the veins to absorb heat and stimulate the flow of blood, while the rest of the wing may perform some other function involving color.

This need for the sun makes butterflies inseparable from the heat of summer. It is why the tropics, with their hot humid climate, abound with magnificent butterflies all year long, while in the mountainous northern areas there are so few butterflies for so short a time.

Butterflies become immobilized at about 40 degrees Fahrenheit. They can remain alive at this temperature for a short time and, when warmth returns, fly and live normally. In climates where the winters are consistently below freezing, however, such a haphazard semi-comatose state will not suffice to carry them through the cold season. They must enter into true hibernation. Over the millenia each genus has evolved its own devices for combatting the cold: some hibernate as eggs, some as butterflies, and others at various stages between.

In New England, the fritillaries lay their eggs in August and September. The eggs hatch, and the newly born caterpillars immediately hibernate. Butterflies from these eggs do not appear until the following July. Members of the genus *Limenitis*, which includes the viceroy, banded purple, and red spotted purple, reach the third larval instar in late August and September. At this

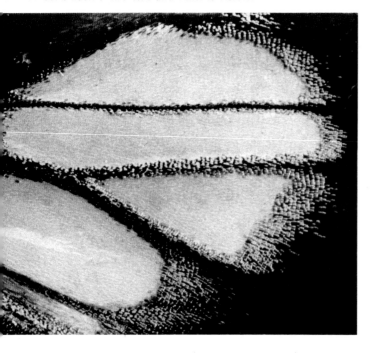

105. *below:* Ctenuchidae, Ecuador. By day the wings of this moth are deeply bordered with dark brown. By moonlight, only an eerie flash of fire-blue and white is visible.

106. *above:* Ctenuchidae. A Cuban moth with narrow elongated wings, thin scaling, and prominent veins.

point they secure one leaf of the food plant to its stem and fashion from it a hooded tube in which they sleep until the following May, crawling forth just as the first leaves are large enough for them to eat. When swallowtail caterpillars reach their full growth, they excrete all the waste materials and excess liquids in their bodies, and become chrysalids in some dark secluded place where their natural camouflage will help to protect them. The species which hibernate as butterflies, such as the tortoise shells and anglewings, emerge from their chrysalids late in summer, seeking out hollow logs, cellarways, porches, or eaves of deserted buildings. Here they hang with their wood-colored wings tightly closed, motionless until the first thawing sun of winter's end calls them back to life.

Hibernating Lepidoptera are able to withstand the cold at 20 degrees below zero—sometimes even lower. During hibernation, with life slowed nearly to a standstill, they can tolerate the most incredible hardships. Caterpillars sleep safely in frozen ground among dead leaves, even covered by slush or freezing water. Chrysalids can survive though buried in six-foot drifts of snow. Butterflies remain alive in their corners and crevices even in the face of blizzards, ice storms, and howling gales. But the monarch, whose body is so geared that it cannot survive a freezing winter at any stage in its life cycle, does not hibernate at all but, like the birds, migrates to a warmer, more inviting place.

Some butterflies will not fly *even in summer* unless the sun is shining brightly. On a day of incidental clouds and light wind, one can watch the common sulphur butterflies popping up from the grass and dropping back again like little

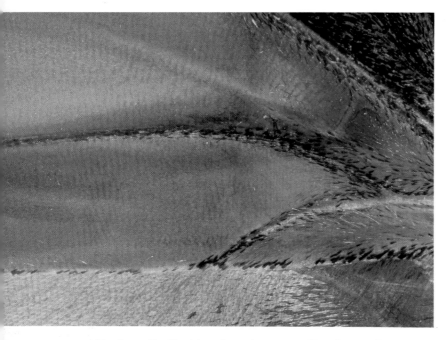

107. *above:* Papilionidae: *Graphium weiski,* New Guinea. This graceful fanlike design is composed of veins at the base of the fore wing. The dark colors of many swallowtail butterflies obscure this lovely pattern.

108. *opposite:* Papilionidae: *Graphium weiski,* New Guinea.

109. *below:* Papilionidae: *Ornithoptera priamus chimaera,* New Guinea. A branching wing vein. The birdwing butterflies are confined in range to the South Sea Islands between New Hebrides and Bataan, with a solitary species *(Ornithoptera priamus euphorion)* occurring on the northern border of Australia.

110. *above:* Nymphalidae: *Limenitis archippus,* United States. Over countless centuries, this butterfly's coloring has evolved until it has now become a nearly perfect mimic of the celebrated monarch. Its closest relatives are mostly black and white with only a few orange markings on the underside.

111. *left:* Pieridae: *Colias cesonia,* United States. There is infinite variety in the wings of butterflies, as is amply shown in the North American Pierids here and in plate 112. The patterns are vastly different, although the arrangement of the veins is similar. Cells of both wings are closed in both species.

112. *below left:* Pieridae: *Anthocaris flora,* United States.

113. *opposite:* Nymphalidae: *Adelpha bredowii,* United States. The veins of this butterfly's wings make a delicate tracery across the irregular pattern of stripes and circles formed by the scales. The open cell of both wings—an important feature in the classification of butterflies—can be clearly seen.

jumping jacks in rhythm to the coming and going of the sun. The Alpine butterfly, *Parnassius apollo*, in contrast to its impetuous flight, literally stops in its tracks the moment the afternoon sun sinks behind the mountains, and can be easily caught between two fingers.

The arrangement of the wing veins is a major factor in determining the genera of both moths and butterflies. All Lepidoptera have the same general vein pattern. All have two strong unbranched veins, the costa and the subcosta, at the front edge of the fore wing. All have a discal cell in both fore wings and hind wings, with several veins radiating from it. In some species the cell is long and thin, in others triangular. It can be heart-shaped; it can be quite irregular. There are also other veins: radius, media, and cubitus—which, with all their branches, total ten—and three anal veins. During fifty million years of evolution, veins have sometimes fused, disappeared partially or entirely, or been reduced to a mere spur. Such slight differences in the condition of the wing veins of a moth or butterfly can give a clue to its place in the process of evolution.

Butterfly wings are of many shapes and sizes. The largest known butterfly is the female *Papilio alexandrae* of New Guinea (Queen Alexandra's birdwing), with wings measuring nearly ten inches from tip to tip. One of the smallest, in Southern California, is the Western pigmy blue (*Brephidium exilis*), which is less than half an inch across. But regardless of shape or size of wings or the part of the world in which any butterfly is found, the venation of the wings is essentially the same for them all.

In summary, the veins function in strengthening the wing, in providing heat, and in defining relationships. The membranes provide a floating surface. The scales are of help in identification of species. Their advantages to the butterfly will be discussed presently. But first—how do the wings work?

## THE MECHANISM OF WINGS

There are three kinds of animals which can fly. If we discount the flying squirrel and the flying fish, which can only glide, the three are bats, birds, and insects. The wings of bats and birds are actually modified legs, just as the flippers of seals and the arms of human beings are modified legs. The wings of butterflies are something entirely different, being formed inside the body, and not appearing as functional appendages until the state of complete maturity has arrived—that is to say, after all the organs of the newly emerged insect, including the wings, wing scales, wing muscles, and wing veins, have reached their ultimate size, shape, and hardness.

I once read the following description of a butterfly: "We now arrive at the Haustellate insects, so called because they suck liquid food through an apparatus resembling the proboscis of an elephant." I shall now try to give an equally colorful description of how the wing of a butterfly operates.

A butterfly's wing in action might be compared to a cross between a seesaw, a sculling oar, and a walking beam of the sort once commonly used on

114. *opposite above:* The mechanism of butterfly wings. Diagrams by Jean Husher.

115. *below:* Papilionidae: *Paride vertumnus,* Trinidad. This plate illustrates the different functions the wings—the fore wings enabl the butterfly to fly, while the hind wings are used for steering.

86

# CROSS SECTION OF MESATHORAX SHOWING HOW
# THE FORE WINGS WORK

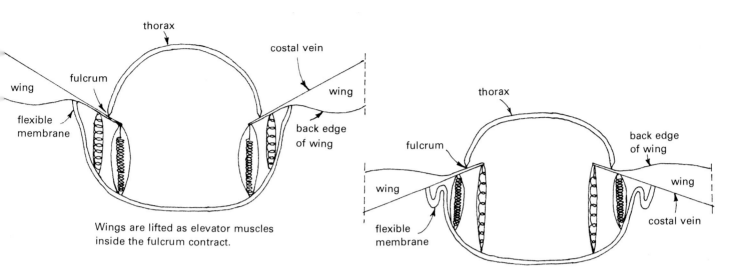

Wings are lifted as elevator muscles
inside the fulcrum contract.

Depressor muscles outside of fulcrum
contract, pulling wing down.

paddle-wheel boats. The wing is attached to, and extends into, the thorax. The point of attachment at the top, or dorsal side of the wing, acts as a fulcrum. Inside the body, a muscle running from the stem end of the wing to the bottom of the thorax pulls the stem down, causing the wing to rise (plate 114, no. 1). The underside of the wing is attached to a flexible membrane which extends outward beyond the fulcrum point. Between this membrane and the fulcrum point, there is another much more powerful muscle which pulls the wing down (plate 114, no. 2). This "walking beam" mechanism produces about nine wing beats a second in a small butterfly—fewer in a large one. It also produces the see-saw motion of the wing. The shape and construction of the wings themselves result in the sculling motion. The strong costal vein on the front edge of the fore wing is rigid, while the softer wing surfaces bend back and forth in response to the air pressure as the wing rises and falls. At the same time, supportive muscles of the thorax vibrate in and out in quick rhythm, enhancing the action of the wings.

The fore wings, supported by the costal veins, enable the insect to fly. If the hind wings are damaged—even badly torn—the insect can still maintain itself in the air. Its flight may be labored and relatively uninteresting, but it can function quite well. Massive damage to one or both of the fore wings, however, is a serious and usually crippling handicap. If one costal vein is broken, the butterfly loses its balance and is unable to leave the ground. If both fore wings should be lost or broken, the hind wings would not be sufficient to lift or support the body in flight.

The function of the hind wings is helping the butterfly to glide, to change speed, and to steer its course. The fore and hind wings cannot be linked together as can the wings of most moths, but there is a rounded flap on the front edge of the butterfly's hind wing which fits behind the fore wing, making it possible for both pairs to function as a unit or separately. Passage of air across or between the wings can be changed according to the position of one pair of wings in relation to the other.

Because of their erratic and seemingly purposeless flight, butterflies have often been used as examples of all that is frivolous and inconsistent. Actually, their instant change of direction, either from side to side or up and down, is a very refined skill which involves all four wings, working in unison or separately. A butterfly's course is a series of unpredictable maneuvers. It baffles and frustrates the lepidopterist but, more important, it ensures escape from all but the most wily and experienced birds. Butterflies with very large wings in comparison to their bodies, such as monarchs, Morphos, and swallowtails, often use the hind wings to sail and glide. The hawk moths, whose wings are small and bodies very large, have less air resistance and are equipped with wing muscles which produce more than seventy strokes a second.

To compare a monarch butterfly with a hawk moth is to compare a seagull with a hummingbird. Each has its own life style. Each is superbly functional in its own environment. The speed and precision of the hawk moth, flying in the semi-dark of evening, makes possible its escape from marauding bats. The monarch can afford to open its enormous wings and glide under a

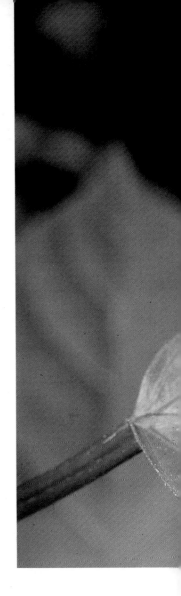

116. Riodinidae: *Crocozona coecias,* Peru. Butterflies mating a patch of sunlight in the jungle.

summer sun because its flame-colored wing scales issue a warning that its body may contain a strong heart poison—a warning that few bird predators will ignore more than once.

## SPECIALIZED SCALES

The scales have achieved so great a diversity that in all probability, like grains of sand, no two are exactly alike. Some scales are still hairlike, but they may be light or dark, stiff or soft, long or short, straight or curly. Some are tactile organs. Some are for display, and for some the *raison d'être* is not yet known.

Some male butterflies have specialized scales which act as perfume dispensers and serve to attract their females at mating time. These scales are called androconia, a Greek word meaning "male dust." Each one contains an infinitesimal tube connected to an endocrine gland and terminating in a microscopic tuft which scatters a pleasing scent. These scales take many forms

89

and occur on various parts of the wings. In the little hairstreaks (genus *Thecla*), they are found in patches on the upper side of the fore wings, but they can also be scattered over the wing surfaces, hidden beneath other scales and impossible to see with the naked eye. Some of the most beautiful, and most elusive, butterflies of South America (*Agrias* and *Prepona*) have a different device. Scent tufts on their hind wings, shaped like bottle brushes but as delicate as spun gold, are displayed during mating.

The birdwing butterflies of the South Pacific islands have a much more complicated organ on the edges of the hind wings closest to the body, the inner margin. Members of one group (*Ornithoptera*) have a thick fringe of long golden hairs on the underside of this margin. In the presence of a female, the wing edge can be turned up and out in a fanlike display as they release their perfume. Another group of birdwings (*Trogonoptera*) has deep invisible pouches on the upper side of the margin. During premating ritual, these pouches open and evert, revealing a cloud of soft ivory-colored floss. In a fold beside the pouch, deeply fringed black scales, lacking in the female, are mingled with iridescent scales. Floss and black scales may somehow be coordinated in the diffusion of perfume, but research has not yet verified this.

The combination of a feathery display and wafted fragrance must be a highly successful approach to mating, since it occurs among butterflies in many parts of the world. Members of the family Danaidae carry out a distinctive, even erotic courtship, involving two separate scent organs. The male has two tiny bundles of hairs called hair pencils hidden in reversible casings at the end of its abdomen. These hairs are sprinkled with microscopic particles of male dust. When partly extruded they resemble minute paint brushes, and when fully open, thistledown, which can be brushed against the antennae of the female. Detailed studies of the queen butterfly (*Danaus gilippus berenice*) have shown that the male is able to raise his abdomen and slap his wings together, pushing the open brushes against a pair of black sex patches on the upper hind-wing surfaces. These patches are thought to be scent receptors containing a waxy substance which retains some of the fragrance.

On the dorsal side of the wings of nearly all male monarchs a day or two old, delightful exotic perfume may be recognized. The fragrance of the monarch is something like a super wild rose. The scents of meadowsweet, verbena, heliotrope, sweetbriar, and many other flowers have been used for describing the scents of various butterflies. It is not hard to imagine why the fragrance of flowers of the field should elicit response from a female newly born, proboscis still untried, who has lived for a fortnight in embryonic darkness. It is more difficult to explain scents like those of chocolate, sandalwood, and orrisroot, which have been attributed to other species.

Interesting as they may be, these special scales are never what most people are thinking about when they say, "There goes a butterfly." They are thinking of all the other scales—the flat overlapping scales—those million specks of glittering colored dust which provide a coat of shining mail for all the glassy membranes of the wings. Human beings see something to marvel at in this lovely display. Butterfly predators are warned and deceived by it.

## SPECIALIZED SCALES

A butterfly's destiny may be controlled in part by the scales of its wings, about which little is known as yet. Most of those shown here still retain an aura of mystery.

117. *left:* Incurvariidae. One scale (magnified 510 times) on the wing of a primitive moth, showing how it is attached to the wing by a ball-and-socket joint. Unlike scales, the minute white hairs (aculeae) are attached directly to the membrane. These hairs are characteristic of two groups of primitive moths.

118. *below:* Papilionidae: *Ornithoptera priamus croesus,* Philippines. Mottled tapestry-like scaling such as this is visible only through a microscope.

119. *above:* Papilionidae: *Papilio krishna,* Sikkim. Velvet black sprinkled with green iridescence colors most of its fore wings, but this butterfly has bands of sparkling blue, purple, green, and pink on its hind wings. A magnified detail of this butterfly (plate 120) shows how the psychedelic effect of the pink areas is produced. Red scales are overlaid with a veneer of lavender reflecting scales, changing to green as the angle of incoming light is changed.

120. *left:* Papilionidae: *Papilio krishna,* Sikkim. Detail of wing.

121. *above:* Pericopidae, Venezuela. The only scales on the wings of this little moth are along the borders and in a single streak crossing the fore wings. Otherwise the wings are clear and the veins clearly visible.

122. *right:* Ithomiidae: *Oleria sp.,* Peru. Butterflies of this genus are often called the starry butterflies, because they "twinkle" in the sun. Excepting for the borders and the cloudy white spots, their wings are transparent. They are also iridescent on the underside, sometimes reflecting a blue or purplish light. (See also plates 6–8.)

123. Papilionidae: *Parnassius phoebus,* United States. Not only tropical but also alpine butterflies can have scaleless areas on their wings. This species is found in the high mountain ranges of the western United States, southern Alaska, and Canada.

124. *above:* Sphingidae, Zululand. The wings of this moth are clad with a thick fur of multiform scales.

125. *right:* Uraniidae: Chrysiridia madagascariensis, Madagascar. Curved scales on the hind wings of this day-flying moth produce a multicolored iridescence when the insect is in flight. Magnified, they resemble a coat of armor.

126. *below:* Papilionidae: *Ornithoptera priamus poseidon,* New Guinea. Dark-toothed scales are hidden beneath suspended iridescent ones and are difficult to see even with a microscope.

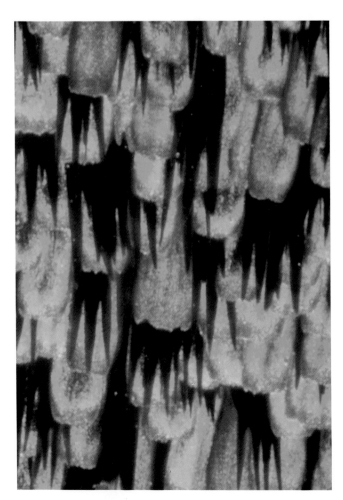

127. *opposite:* Papilionidae: *Trogonoptera trojanus,* Philippines. Jagged black scales are found in a fold of the hind wing of the males of the *trojanus* group, but not of the females. They probably function in the dissipation or storage of perfume during the pre-mating ritual.

128. *above:* Pieridae: *Colias eurydice,* United States. Iridescence can be clearly seen on the fore wings of this familiar dog-faced butterfly.

131. *opposite:* Papilionidae: *Ornithoptera priamus croesus,* Philippines. The males of the *priamus* group of birdwings have a golden fringe along the inner margin of the hind wing, which can be turned upward and so displayed at mating time. It is part of a scent-producing mechanism.

129. *above:* Papilionidae: *Parides photinus,* Mexico. Pouches on the hind wings of this and a number of other male swallowtails unfold during courtship to reveal a mass of fluffy scent scales.

130. *right:* Lycaenidae: *Thecla syncellus,* Colombia. This photograph shows the scent spot on the right fore wing of the male butterfly; in this species it is composed of three groups of specialized scales. The scent organs of most male butterflies are on the hind wings or at the end of the abdomen.

132. *left:* Pyralidae, Uruguay. Moths as well as butterflies can have extensible scent brushes. In this picture of a small moth, they are fully extended.

133. *below:* Nymphalidae: *Agrias narcissus,* Brazil. Extensible golden plumes of scent scales are located near the inner margins of the hind wings of all males of the genera *Agrias* and *Prepona,* which exude perfume to attract the females and add a shining ornament to butterflies widely considered to rank among the world's most spectacular species.

134. *opposite:* Incurvariidae. The Incurvariidae are a very primitiv family of micro-moths, which retains certain characteristics thought to have been present in some of the earliest true moths. According to recent discoveries, moths must have appeared on th earth at least one hundred million years ago, for in the Cretaceou deposits in Manitoba, Canada, one lone fossil caterpillar was foun which is judged to be over ninety-five million years old, and sever fossil moths have been gleaned from the oil shales of Utah and Wyoming. The photographs for this and the following three plate taken with an electron scanning microscope, are of moths measuring no more than two centimeters from wing tip to wing tip

This plate shows the eye, the proboscis partly uncurled, and th base of one antenna, magnified 36 times. In this moth the antenna are about the same length as the wings. Some members of the family have incredibly long antennae which trail behind them whe they fly.

# The Compound Eye

Scientists have studied the compound eyes of insects since the beginning of the nineteenth century. Innumerable treatises have been written on the subject. Many diagrams—and more recently photographs—have exposed their hidden complexities, but we still have no clear idea of what a butterfly really sees.

The eye of a butterfly is among the most intricate of all known mechanisms by which animals see. The human eye, with its single lens and single retina, is simple indeed by comparison. The butterfly's eye, like the human eye, is covered by a cornea, but the corneal layer in a butterfly is composed of thousands of contiguous double convex lenses, through each of which light passes. Beneath each of these lenses is a crystal cone which tapers inwardly to form a transparent rod. By the time the light reaches this rod, it has been reversed twice and its rays have become parallel, so that it enters the rod in a straight line.

Attached to and surrounding the rod is a rhabdom. This is a cluster of six or eight elongated visual cells which extend to the base of the eye, each ending

in a network of incredibly minute nerve fibrils. Together these fibrils comprise nerve fibers, each of which is, in turn, part of the optic nerve.

The complete unit described here so briefly is known as an omatidium; of these there are six thousand beneath the cornea of each eye—one for every corneal lens. Each omatidium is separated from those adjacent to it by a curtain of pigment, so that only direct light can reach the base of each cone and be transmitted to the brain. Light rays reaching one cone cannot be transmitted sideways to another, since all oblique light is absorbed by the pigment cells. Moths, which fly at night or at dusk, are endowed with a mechanism that shrinks or expands the pigment cells as the visual needs of the moth change.

The shape and structure of its compound eyes enable the butterfly to see in all directions except directly beneath its body. Does it see, then, a nearly spherical image, distorted as in a convex or concave mirror? Or does it see a panorama? A mosaic? A composite picture like those currently being taken of the moon's surface? At what distance will each omatidium produce an image in focus? Is a part of what these elegant compound eyes perceive always blurred?

135. Incurvariidae. The eye and surrounding petal-like scales, magnified 160 times.

*Opposite:*
136. Incurvariidae. When one s◌ hairlike projection, with its surrounding omatidia, is magni◌ 1920 times, it appears to be sea◌ in a microscopic cornucopia, an◌ the omatidia are shown to have ◌ granular surface.

137. Incurvariidae. A section of ◌ omatidium enlarged 19,800 tim◌ covering approximately two square centimeters of the previ◌ picture. This grainy surface probably prevents excessive amounts of light from entering ◌ eye. The eyes of mammals are similarly protected by blinking l◌ which distribute a film of moist◌ over the eyeball.

With the electron scanning microscope, new mysteries have been brought to light. It has now been discovered that between the double convex lenses of the cornea are scattered hitherto invisible hairs—sensory hairs, perhaps, but their function is not yet known. It has also been found that the surface of each double convex lens is not smooth, but covered with granules of a smallness far beyond the limits of the imagination. Such granules must diffuse the light; they may perhaps have the same function that moisture has for lidded eyes— that of preventing too much light from entering.

Can a butterfly distinguish objects? Shapes? Is what it sees in perspective? In proportionate size? Even these questions we can answer only in part. We know that a butterfly perceives motion from all sides, and that this enables it to avoid many dangers. We also know—for many experiments have proved it —that butterflies can see and distinguish between colors to a remarkable degree. For instance, it is the habit of many butterflies to establish territorial rights by chasing other males away from their chosen area. Some of the great blue Morphos which inhabit the tops of the rain forests can be lured to within a few feet of the ground by a scrap of blue silk tethered to a long pole, which they attack as they would another male.

In one experiment, the behavior of the pearl-bordered fritillary (*Argynnis euphrosyne*), a British butterfly, was studied. Dead specimens, some bleached and re-dyed, some in their natural state, and paper replicas of the same species were pinned to leaves in a field where the butterfly normally flies. Time after time the live insects approached and even touched the lures with colors and patterns most like their own tawny orange wings. They paid little attention to those painted brown or buff, and completely ignored all with drastically different colors such as blue, green, chartreuse, and pale yellow.

If butterflies react to color to this extent, then color must play a part in the ceremony of mating; and there is evidence that it does for both males and females. When males are establishing a territory, for instance, they will drive

138. *below left:* Sphingidae. Simple eyes on one side of the head of an Argentinian sphinx caterpillar greatly magnified. These eyes enable it to see light probably to tell what direction sun is coming from.

139. *below right:* Papilionidae: *Trogonoptera trojanus,* Philippines. A detail of the eye this tropical birdwing butterfly shows about 600 of the 6000 lens of which each eye is composed Beneath each lens are six crystal cones, each connected to the brain by a nerve. Each eye consequently has 36,000 units of sight.

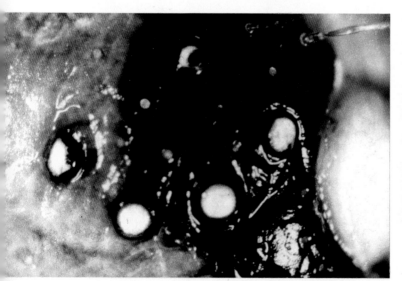

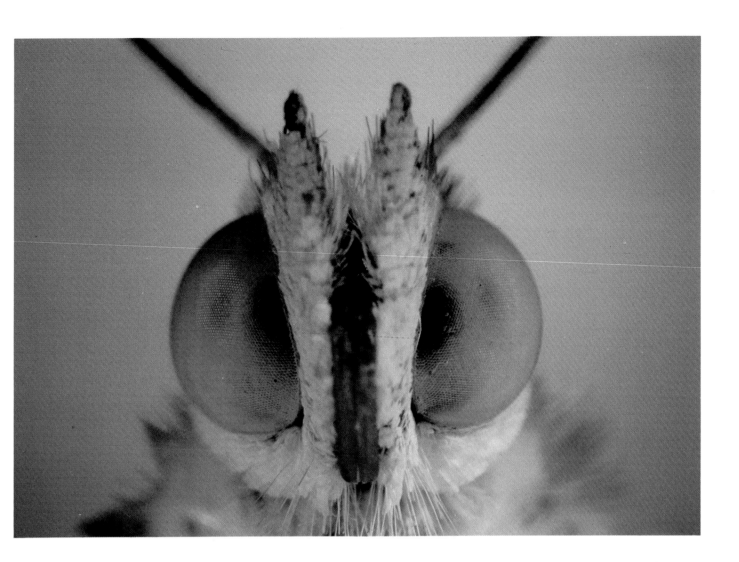

0. *above:* Pieridae: *Pieris rapae,* ...ited States. Curled proboscis, ...lpi, and eyes of the most ...evalent of United States ...tterflies. These eyes can see ...ht in the ultraviolet range, which ...ay help males in choosing a mate.

away other males of their own species, in the manner of birds. Other experiments have shown that males of some species have difficulty in attracting a mate if the color has been removed from their wings.

The wings of female butterflies pose a tantalizing enigma, because they often diverge radically from the expected color norm. Females of some species do not resemble their males at all. The tropical American Morphos and most of the birdwing butterflies of the South Sea Islands fall into this category. The orange and yellow sulphurs (genus *Colias*) each has females like the males and white females as well. The tiger swallowtail (*Papilio turnus*), a large yellow and black butterfly, is found in the Eastern United States. In the North, the male and female are similar, but in the South, the female assumes two forms—one yellow like the male, and the other almost totally black. Even Linneaus at first thought that the black form was a new species and gave it the name *Papilio glaucus.* Research has shown that the southern males show a definite preference for the females which are bright yellow like themselves, but they readily mate with the dark melanic females in areas where these outnumber the yellow females. As a complicating factor, there are at least four other black butterflies similar in size, shape, and pattern to the black *turnus* female. Does the male choose his mate by color or not? Are the males able to discriminate to a remarkable degree between small color differences? Or are additional factors present, such as scent and behavior patterns, which enable both males and females to recognize their own species regardless of wing color? Alas, in the fabric of nature, no thread follows so simple a path as "either/or."

It has recently been discovered that on the wings of certain butterflies of the family Pieridae, there are special scales which reflect ultraviolet light. Also, it has been demonstrated that, unlike human beings, butterflies are able to see light in the ultraviolet range. With the discovery of this special gift, hidden from human intelligence for so long, a whole new field of research has been opened, and a new light shed upon some of the most vexing problems of insect behavior.

The white cabbage butterfly (*Pieris rapae*) is a case in point (plate 140). The wings of the female, but not the male, reflect ultraviolet light. Many fascinating experiments with this prevalent little butterfly have shown that the underside of the wings of the female, visible when they are closed, is the most attractive to the male. Yet ultraviolet light reflected from the underside is less intense than that from the upper surfaces, which the male tends to ignore. So it seems that the *brilliance* of ultraviolet reflectance is not what attracts the male, but rather certain *wave lengths* of it. Within the scope of these wave lengths, the amount of reflected light may be altered by the quality of the sunlight at a given time of day or time of year, and also by the concentration of reflecting scales in a given wing area. One can only marvel that invisible stimuli as esoteric as these exist—and perhaps exist for no other purpose than to ensure the continuation of a species! The colors visible to the male are probably unlike anything which the human eye can see. In sun or shadow, we see these little butterflies only as scraps of white or creamy yellow. The male butterflies may see the females glittering with fuchsia or psychedelic purples. No means has yet been devised to reproduce for us those colors beyond the range of visible light, but the ability to see and to distinguish them from plain pigmented colors is an ordinary skill of the most common butterfly in the world.

# Protective Devices

The diversity of color in female butterflies in general has, to date, seemed even more closely related to protection than to sexual behavior. Obviously, deceit by color is only a small part of the total system of interlocking checks and balances by which all species maintain viable relationships. All species must eat to live, and therefore all species must be eaten. Protection must be good enough to insure the continuation of life, but not good enough to allow any one species to dominate its environment to the point of starving out or otherwise eliminating all the other species. Periodically one species or another may threaten to become dominant because its food plant becomes abundant and its predators and parasites become scarce. Under such conditions its population soon reaches proportions which the decimated predators fail to control, and which the food supply is unable to sustain. The result is hysterical behavior, such as the lemmings' trek to the sea, which results in the loss of great numbers of individuals. The results of hysteria are not as disastrous to some creatures as to the lemmings. Winged insects can often fly fast enough and far enough to find other food before becoming exhausted. When locusts embark on such a mass exodus, the disaster is to crops and people, although advantages to individual participating locusts are short-lived.

Some butterflies—the fast fliers whose wing muscles are exceptionally strong—also make these one-way migrations. The painted lady (*Vanessa cardui*), the red admiral (*V. atalanta*), the tropical American tailed flambeau (*Marpesia petreus*), and the Venezuelan shoemaker (*Historis acheronta*) are among them. These migrations serve a dual purpose: one, the butterflies may reach an un-tapped food source, and two, the new area may be one which has not yet been invaded by their specific parasites. Therefore, for a while they can live in rela-tive safety in a land of plenty. But the forces governing cyclical change are never really stilled. Butterfly numbers multiply, and larval food supply is ravaged. More birds come to feast on a bumper crop of caterpillars. Parasites also increase, and butterfly numbers diminish. Season on season, eccentric weather changes tip the balance slightly in favor of one form of life or another. Eventually a season will come when all the whims of weather and all the changes in environment will be aligned to produce butterflies in epidemic numbers. With this day, the butterflies will embark on another migration. Hundreds of thousands of individuals will die *en route*, but a few will reach some distant place where their offspring, like their ancestors, can flourish for a brief span. And so, both migration and decimation of numbers contribute to the survival of the species.

Fluctuation is a ceaseless part of the evolutionary process. Along with it, many protective devices have been and are always being developed to ensure the survival of many different species, not just one. All creatures must adapt to new circumstances, and butterflies, frail as they are, have done so for over seventy million years. But on a day when new larval food supplies no longer exist, even in distant places, the migrating species dependent upon them may well face extinction.

Protective coloration is a vitally important function of the wing scales—a matter of life and death in a very real sense. It can be achieved in several ways. First, there is camouflage, or disruptive coloration, which permits the butterfly to "disappear" into its background. Second, there is warning colora-tion, acting like a red flag or flashing yellow light. Third, there is mimicry, in which one butterfly receives protection by looking like another or like some other animal.

When butterflies and moths are at rest, the fore wings cover the dorsal, or upper, side of the hind wings. But since butterflies rest with wings closed over their backs, it is the underside of the hind wings which is visible. Moths rest with wings open, and the upper side of the fore wings is visible. When camou-flage occurs, its function is to protect the insect while at rest, and hence the underside of the hind wings of butterflies and the upper side of the fore wings of moths are the parts always so protected.

Perhaps the only case in which the camouflage of a Lepidopteron has been wholly changed during a period shorter than the life span of a human being is the now classic case of the peppered moth of Great Britain (*Biston butelaria*). This moth, normally white with black markings, was perfectly cam-

1. Notodontidae. Against pale
~rk on a dead tree, this moth is
~tually invisible.

ouflaged when resting on the trunks of birch trees. It was, however, native to
an area which became heavily industrialized. The smoke from the factories
caused the birch bark to become blackened, and in less than three quarters of
a century the moths also became black to match the trees. The agent for
change was the predatory birds, which, as the trees gradually darkened, discovered the lightest moths and ate them. The slightly darker moths escaped to
mate, and gradually the dark genes became dominant. The same moth in
country areas is still white.

Many more moths than butterflies are protected by tree camouflage of
this sort, since moths often rest on tree bark during the day in full view of vast

142. *left:* Limacodidae. Hanging by the front feet.

143. *below:* Notodontidae. Rolling up like a dead leaf.

144. *above:* Zanolidae. Standing on its head.

145. *right:* Mimallonidae. Spreading against a tree trunk.

numbers of hungry birds (plate 141). But "the art of vanishing" is a widespread device among insects. For those butterflies which hibernate in the adult stage and must remain motionless all winter, it is indispensable. Both hind wings and fore wings can be camouflaged. If they are, this seemingly double protection is related to the fact that some butterflies rest with the underside of both fore wings and hind wings showing. The leaf butterfly of India (*Kallima inachus*) is the outstanding example of this kind of posturing, having developed the most perfect of all butterfly camouflage, but butterflies all over the world are effectively hidden by their leaflike or barklike wing scaling. The question sign (*Polygonia interrogationis*) is perhaps our most leaflike butterfly. Streaks of dark scales on the underside of both wings, the irregular shape of the wing margins, and the short stemlike tails of the hind wings all serve to disguise it against any backdrop of faded leaves.

Tree camouflage is not all dull brown and gray. The tiger swallowtails are dramatically visible when flying in a meadow or drinking at a roadside puddle, but if they sail into the branches of a tree, black streaks on the pale gold of their wings cause them to melt completely away in a background of filtered sunlight. Each species has its own peculiar way of disappearing and its own special habits for using its camouflage to the best advantage. The little European hairstreak, *Callophrys rubi*, is dull brown on the dorsal side—emerald green and iridescent below. It alights on low-growing juniper and leans to one side, orienting its wings to match the sunlight on its background. The list is endless. There is no more refreshing occupation on a summer's day than strolling in a meadow and watching the butterflies vanish and reappear as they carry out their untroubled routine of flower visiting, resting, escaping, courting, and mating. Acting by instinct only, and oblivious to danger, a butterfly in action is the happy antithesis of today's world of anxiety and problems.

Our common northern milkweed (*Asclepias syriaca*) belongs to a large family of plants, many of which contain substances known as cardiac glycosides. These glycosides are poisonous to birds.

Milkweeds are the food not only of the monarch caterpillar but, as far as is known, of all members of the family Danaidae to which the monarch belongs. This includes species from Malaysia, Thailand, many parts of Africa, North and South America, and Australia. The caterpillars which eat the poisonous kinds of milkweed ingest the poisons and retain them, so that when they become butterflies they are still poisonous. A bird which eats a poisonous Danaid has much the same reaction as a man who encounters a skunk; he avoids any similar contact in the future. As an adjunct to this protection, many Danaids have developed distinctive wing colors which act as a warning signal to birds. The monarch, with its flame-colored wings, jet-black wing veins, and striking black and white wing tips, is the best-known example. A bird could hardly miss this warning signal, especially since the monarch flaunts its colors by flying in long slow glides with open wings.

The milkweed plants most prevalent in the northern parts of the United States (*Asclepias syriaca*, *A. tuberosa*, *A. incarnata*) apparently do not contain components which are poisonous to birds. Therefore, it would seem that the

109

146. *below:* Gelechiidae. Many small moths are able to emulate broken twigs by settling on appropriately patterned trees and rolling their wings around their bodies, as shown here and in plates 147 and 148.

147. *right:* Notodontidae.

148. *below:* Notodontidae.

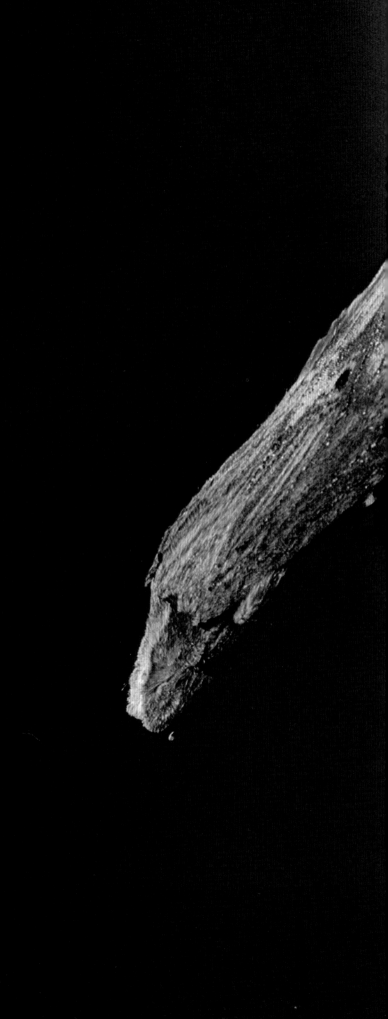

149. *inset above right:* Sphingidae, Venezuela. This Sphingid may lose much of its green color when its wings have hardened, but against green moss on a tree trunk it is camouflaged until ready to fly.

150. *inset below right:* Yponomeutidae. This small moth has rolled his wings across his back, imitating a beetle.

151. *left:* Noctuidae. Cryptic pattern is part of the protective coloration of this moth.

152. *right:* Noctuidae. Outline, coloring, and position combine to give this moth the appearance of being a knothole.

monarch eggs laid on these milkweeds in New England and Canada would produce nontoxic butterflies. If this is true, how can these monarchs be protected by their warning colors? It is well known that the monarch is a true migrant, traveling from Canada to Florida or California, and even to Mexico and Central and South America. A northern migration begins in late February or early March, and the first monarchs again arrive in New England in late May.

The population movements of this butterfly are very complex and, despite a massive banding program, far from thoroughly understood. However, there are many reasons to believe that the monarchs which arrive in New England in the spring are not the same ones which traveled south the previous fall. During the winter some of the band of fall migrants apparently go into semi-hibernation and do not mate until just before the spring migration begins. Others continue to breed during the winter. Some may remain in the south for several generations without migrating. There may be South American monarchs which never migrate at all or which never go farther north than Mexico.

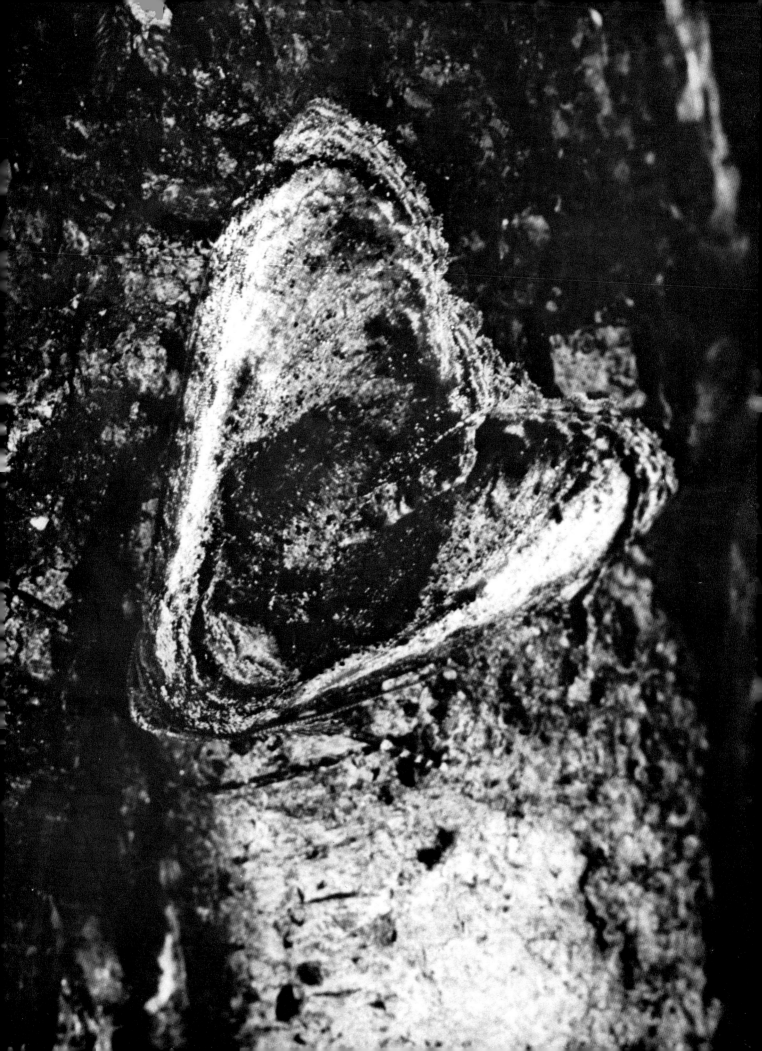

153. *left:* Nymphalidae: *Colobura dirce,* Brazil. Sucking moisture from the trunk of a dead tree, this butterfly is clearly visible. In a tangle of jungle growth, lighted by filtered sun, it can be nearly invisible.

154. *below left:* Nymphalidae: *Agrias sardanapalus,* Peru. The underside of the butterfly in plate 155, revealing a row of glaring eyes. It may be protected more, though, by its warning coloration than by its rather small eyespots. The somewhat cryptic pattern is also part of its protective coloration.

155. *below:* Nymphalidae: *Agrias sardanapalus,* Peru. This is one of the most spectacular and, because of its rarity and the difficulty of catching it, one of the most sought-after butterflies in the world.

156. *left:* Danaidae: *Danaus plexippus,* United States. A female monarch feeds peacefully. The male in the background has lost part of a hind wing, probably to a predatory bird, which then rejected as distasteful. In plate 157 a second male has arrived, chased away the first male, and mated with the female. She is now suspended quiescently beneath him while he feeds peacefully.

157. *right:* Danaidae: *Danaus plexippus,* United States.

In any case, a majority of monarch caterpillars found from Florida southward are apt to be feeding on either of the two most prevalent tropical varieties of milkweed (*Asclepias curissavica, A. humistrata*), both of which contain large amounts of the glycosides which are toxic to birds.

The overwintering nontoxic butterflies which mate at winter's end lay their eggs on their way north and probably die before they have gone very far. The eggs which they deposit on the poisonous tropical milkweeds will produce poisonous butterflies, and these poisonous butterflies will presumably reach the northern limits of the migration. *Their* eggs, laid on northern milkweed, will produce nontoxic butterflies, but they will be protected by the fact that birds have already experienced the first incoming wave of poisonous butterflies.

They will avoid the second edible brood, which looks exactly like the first.

This is an admittedly simplistic discussion of a very complicated problem, but perhaps it serves to illustrate in a small way the interdependence of species, the ebbing and flowing, the interlocking puzzle that is life. For in September and October of some years, thousands of monarch butterflies gather in fields of goldenrod, gliding up and down like a shower of gold; they congregate in trees in a shimmering mass in late afternoon. And although they are presumably edible, they are almost entirely free from predation by birds.

Warning coloration and mimicry are so closely related that it is not really possible to consider one without the other. The warning colors of the monarch constitute only a minor part of this alliance, for Danaids in all parts of the world where they occur are protected by poisons and mimicked by other species edible to birds. The monarch, as is well known, is mimicked by the viceroy (*Limenitis archippus*). The African swallowtail (*Papilio dardanus*) has at least seven female forms, only one of which is like the male. The others all mimic various Danaids of the genus *Amauris*.

There are only three species of Danaids in the United States. There are at least fourteen species in Africa, where they breed continuously and are on the wing throughout the year over most of their range. In a region whose climate permits year-round, continuous breeding and where the food plant is exceptionally toxic, mimicry can develop in a relatively short time. *Danaus chrysippus* (the African monarch), has, itself, three distinct forms, all of which are mimicked by nonpoisonous butterflies, including swallowtails, Nymphalids, and at least one Lycaenid. One African swallowtail has three female forms, each mimicking one of the forms of *Danaus chrysippus*, and a fourth which mimics an entirely different species of Danaid. This phenomenon is called sexual polymorphism. The divergent females may all look like other species of butterflies, but the likenesses are actually superficial. Some can be brought about by a single gene change. In most cases these changes affect only the wing scaling.

No one has yet discovered how many mimics there are for the family as a whole, nor how many butterflies simply gain protection by bearing a chance resemblance to the noxious Danaids without actually being true mimics; nor how many of the butterflies still in doubt may be in the process of evolving into mimics.

The mimicry of a toxic species such as the Danaids by a nontoxic species is known as Batesian mimicry (plates 153, 156). This type of mimicry evolves through natural selection over many years. It can evolve only in places where the toxic model is more prevalent than a nontoxic butterfly with similar characteristics, since, according to the law of averages, a predatory bird has more chances to try the more numerous toxic species first.

Roughly, this is how Batesian mimicry works. A bird that eats a toxic butterfly becomes violently ill; it does not die but soon recovers. The toxic butterfly attacked or eaten does die, but the whole species or whole colony gains protection by the sacrifice of a single individual, because, having recovered, the bird thereafter associates the colors and/or pattern of the toxic butterfly with its bad effects and avoids similar colors and patterns in choosing its prey.

158. Danaidae: *Danaus chrysippus* (form *alchippus*), West Africa. This is the model for a great many African mimics. The other two forms lack the large white area on the hind wings.

Since a bird that has been poisoned avoids any butterfly resembling the toxic species, palatable species with colors or patterns similar to the toxic species are spared and individuals least like the toxic species are eaten. Thus the individuals most like the toxic model—the butterflies that carry genes for warning colors and patterns—are left to breed and they mate until those genes become dominant. This selective process eventually results in nearly perfect mimicry.

There are other butterflies besides the Danaids which are poisonous, evil-smelling, or nauseating. Like the Danaids, all of these butterflies have their mimics. As far as is known, all butterflies so protected feed as caterpillars upon plants with distasteful or poisonous juices. In the United States the black female of the eastern tiger swallowtail and four other southern butterflies are mimics of the poisonous pipe-vine swallowtail, which gains its protection by feeding upon various Aristolochiae in the larval stage (plates 154, 155).

The Heliconians, many of which resemble the monarch in color and pattern, are a large family of tropical butterflies which inhabit the rain forests of

159. Nymphalidae: *Speyeria dia* (male), United States. The colori of the male butterfly here is simi to that of other members of the genus. The female in plate 160 is striking black with iridescent blu hind wings. It is thought that this one of several butterflies which mimic the poisonous pipe-vine swallowtail, thereby gaining protection from predatory birds The monarch *(Danaus plexippu* and the viceroy *(Limenitis archippus)* belong to another su mimicry complex.

120

South America. In the larval stages they all feed on passion vines, which are poisonous plants, and the butterflies are also poisonous. They are warningly marked, usually in patterns combining red and black or orange and black with white or pale yellow. The Heliconians remain fairly close to the place of their emergence, several species often cohabiting the same area and all mimicking one another, often so perfectly that only an expert can tell them apart by wing pattern alone. They are also mimicked by certain female Pierids (the sulphurs and whites). The Heliconians share their habitat with butterflies of another distasteful family, the Ithomiidae, of which they are co-mimics.

The co-mimicry of two or more toxic species is known as Müllerian mimicry (plates 20, 78, 157). Like Batesian mimicry, it evolves by natural selection. Butterflies are made toxic by eating poisonous plants during their larval stages. The larvae do not digest the toxic substances in the plants but store, or sequester, them during metamorphosis, causing the butterflies to become toxic also. When several species of butterflies having the same larval food plant cohabit in the

same area, the most toxic becomes the most successful by natural selection, and the others, also by natural selection, evolve to mimic it. Since they all fly together during the day and roost together in large congregations during the night, the sacrifice of a few again protects the whole colony.

To add to the complications, Heliconians of the same species inhabiting different parts of the rain forest often bear little resemblance to each other, and can only be sorted out by a study of the caterpillar stages and genitalia. There are actually some species which are red and black in one area and bright iridescent blue in another. And in each area they may all mimic or be mimicked by other Heliconians, other Ithomiids, or other Pierids, the last of which are nontoxic but gain protection by Batesian mimicry! Sometimes only the female Pierid is mimetic—sometimes both sexes are. This situation is so complex that the most experienced experts are the least likely to attempt an identification without a detailed examination of each individual insect.

A fourth family of poisonous butterflies is the Acraeidae of Africa, but the complications here are truly monumental, for in Africa south of the Sahara there are about 2,500 known species of butterflies. For many of them the larval and chrysalis stages are as yet unknown.

The tropics are still a butterfly paradise, but for the lepidopterist they are a tantalizing enigma. Tragically, the tropical forests with their lush vegetation and unique fauna are fast being developed. Modern methods and the lure of quick profit make it expedient to level the trees and strip the land without regard for the animals, plants, and insects that will be forever destroyed. In a short time—surely within the lifetime of most people alive today—the rain forests and the marvelous panorama of butterflies they harbor will no longer exist.

It must have taken millions of years for these butterflies to attain the perfect disguise which they enjoy today, with the warning colors of both model and mimic developing more or less simultaneously by natural selection. Acquiring the scale colors and wing patterns of another flying creature is not at all the same as matching a stationary tree. Mimicry must have been painfully achieved by countless trials and errors, for according to the law of averages, many birds must have eaten an edible butterfly before encountering its inedible model—especially in the early eons when wing patterns were not very distinctive. The time schedule, habitat, climate, food, and numbers of all species involved—birds, butterflies, and plants—must have first arrived at nearly perfect coordination. And all these things must have happened around the world time after time, eon after eon, for mimicry to have become so prevalent and so perfected.

We have seen how wing scaling can result in camouflage, and how the butterfly uses this camouflage to the best advantage by closing its wings, and the moth by folding its fore wings over its hind wings when at rest. It may be that an entirely different device, a sort of entomological masquerade, has been evolved principally to protect the insect during those two or three perilous hours after its wings have attained their full size, but before it is ready to fly. At this time, if a butterfly is touched, it will suddenly open its wings, flashing

162. Acraeidae: *Acraea encedon,* West Africa. This butterfly and
*Danaus chrysippus* are both poisonous and are mutually mimetic.

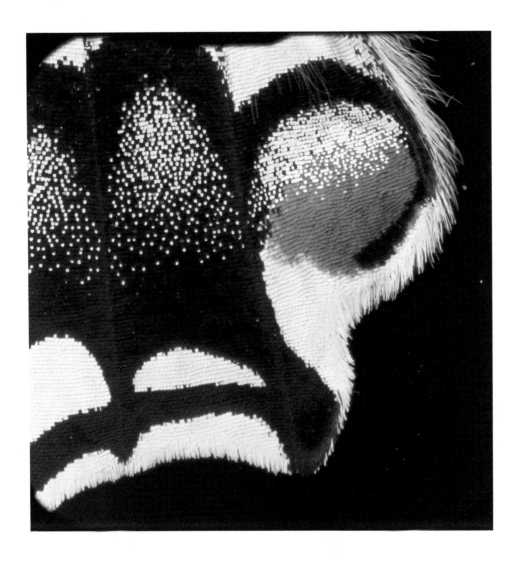

163. *left:* Papilionidae: *Papilio machaon,* France. Detail of eyespot. *Machaon* can be identified by the fact that the red eyespot has no black spot within it

the upper surface in the face of the intruder. At other times in its life if a butterfly is touched, or even approached, it will dart away as the collector well knows. But it cannot escape from a predatory bird before its wings are thoroughly hardened. Therefore, this sudden flashing of colors must at that time be an essential life-saving act. This is probably why, during the course of evolution, certain butterflies and moths have acquired on the upper surface of their hind wings large spots bearing a remarkable resemblance to the eyes of birds and animals (plate 174). Some are large round spots or rings, while others have shadings, irises, and pupils, and still others glassy unscaled areas which reflect light like real eyes. It is a well-known fact that birds respond with symptoms of alarm to these spots when they appear suddenly as if out of nowhere. The more eyelike the spot, the more violent the response of the bird. In addition, birds have a habit of pecking at an object before eating it, which could provide the stimulus for the wings to open. Among the Lepidoptera in our fauna, the buckeye (*Precis lavinia*) and its relatives, the polyphemus moth (*Telea polyphemus*) and other Saturnid moths, are protected in this way. There

164. *below:* Papilionidae: *Papilio machaon,* Alaska. One of the
largest European butterflies and a close relative of many North
American species, notably *Papilio polyxenes,* the black swallowtail of
the East Coast, and *Papilio zolicaon,* its western counterpart.
*Machaon* is found in Alaska and the Yukon.

165. *opposite:* Nymphalidae: *Precis orithya,* China.

166. *above right:* Nymphalidae: *Nymphalis io,* France. This butterfly's large blue eyespots have earned it the nickname of "peacock."

167. Nymphalidae: *Precis artaxia,* Malawi. Butterflies of this genus occur in many parts of the world, and all have rows of prominent eyespots on the edges of their wings—a deterrent to predatory birds.

168. Nymphalidae: *Prepona praeneste,* Peru. Formidable though they may look here, the eyespots on the underside of the hind wing of *Prepona* species are in reality only about the size of a half-carat diamond.

169. Nymphalidae: *Prepona eugenes,* Peru.

170. Nymphalidae: *Prepona krates,* Peru.

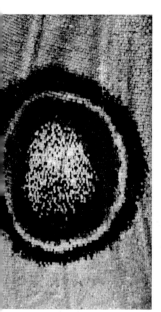
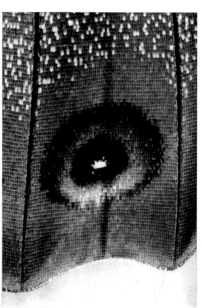

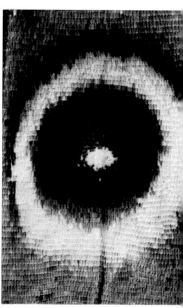

171. *opposite:* Brassolidae: *Caligo martia,* Brazil. Butterflies of the genus *Caligo* are dark blue, purple, or brown on the dorsal side, but on the underside all are mottled brown with a pair of large eyespots on the hind wings. This specimen is posed to show its remarkable resemblance to an owl's head. In nature, the butterfly flies only at dusk, as its eyes cannot stand the bright sun. When it settles on the trunk of a tree during the day, it rests with closed wings, so that only one of the eyes can be seen at a time. However, one is enough to warn off bird predators, who are understandably wary of owls at any time of day.

172. *above:* Brassolidae: *Caligo sp.,* Venezuela. Members of the genus *Caligo* are called owl butterflies because, with open wings, the underside of the hind wings has the appearance of an owl's head. One such eyespot is sufficient to frighten a bird away, and it can be made to appear very suddenly when the butterfly snaps its wings together.

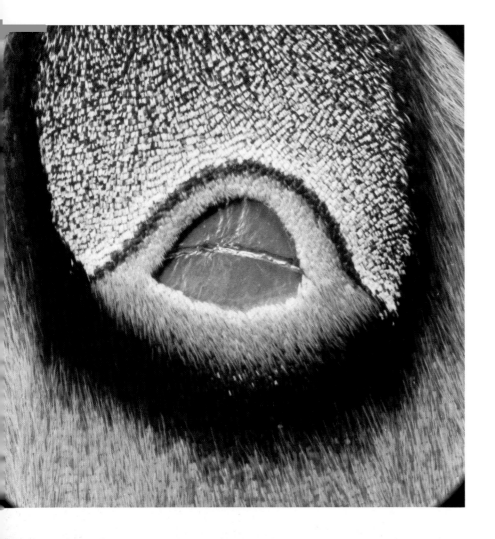

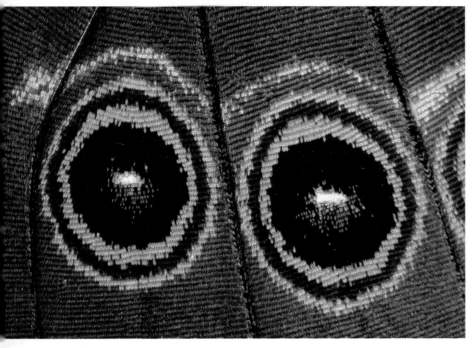

173. *left:* Saturniidae: *Telea polyphemus,* United States. The "pupil" of the eyespot of the polyphemus moth is unscaled and therefore transparent. In this photograph a blue background can be seen through it.

174. *above:* Saturniidae, Africa. Some eyespots, like those of this Rhodesian moth, are formed by shining unscaled areas surrounded by thick hairlike scales. Unscaled areas reflect light like a mirror. Many Saturnids have such decorative eyespots on their fore wings.

175. *left:* Morphidae: *Morpho achilles,* Peru. The underside of the wings of Morpho butterflies lack iridescence, are protectively colored, and are usually decorated with glaring eyespots.

176. *opposite:* Nymphalidae: *Megistanis baeotus,* Brazil. Eyespots and short bright tails draw the attention of predators away from the butterfly's body. This cryptically marked insect has both.

is a difference between this kind of protection and that achieved by butterflies of the genus *Caligo*. These huge South American butterflies are blue on the upper surface, but have one large owlish "eye" on the *underside* of each hind wing, clearly visible only when the butterfly is resting.

One more device of the wings needs to be mentioned, because it protects the butterfly by attracting its enemies instead of repelling them. There are "tails" on the hind wings of various species, notably the swallowtails, sword-tails, and hairstreaks in our fauna, and throughout the world. The luna moth and several other Saturnids also have conspicuous tails, the most unusual being the males of a South American moth of the genus *Copeopteryx,* whose tails are five inches long—four times the length of their bodies! Many members of the Malaysian family Amathiisidae also have short tails or angular pointed hind wings. The Mexican swallowtail, *Papilio pilimnus,* has three sets of hind-wing projections, as does the day-flying moth of Madagascar, *Chrysiridia madagas-cariensis.* These tails actually lure birds away from the more vulnerable portions of the body. This is why tailed species so often are seen with their tails damaged or missing. Birds are attracted by the projecting tails when the butterfly is in flight and snap them off, missing the palatable body. Some tails are made more alluring by small spots located on or near them. Many swallow-tails have conspicuous red or red-and-black spots on the lower edges of their

177. *above:* Papilionidae: *Bhutanitis lidderdalei,* Philippine Large eyespots combined with quadruple tails give this butterfly an altogether spectacular appearance.

134

8. *right:* Lycaenidae: *Syntarucus sp.,* Malawi. [th]is combination of eyespots and tail produces [a c]omical effect in this small Lycaenid.

[8]9. *below:* Papilionidae: *Papilio cresphontes,* [Un]ited States. *Cresphontes* has been taken as [as] north as Massachusetts and as far west as [Mi]nnesota and the Mexican border, but it is [mo]st abundant in areas where citrus fruits are [gr]own (but not sprayed).

[ ] The United States is rich in swallowtails. At [lea]st twenty-one species of true swallowtails [oc]cur in the area east of the Mississippi alone, [co]mpared to only three species between the [Da]rdanelles and the North Cape in Europe. [ ]Tails vary greatly in length, from an almost [in]visible stub *(Papilio polydamus)* to a trailing [tail] nearly as long as the hind wing *(Graphium [m]arcellus).* The tails of *cresphontes* are rather [sh]ort, but bright yellow tips make them appear [lon]ger in flight.

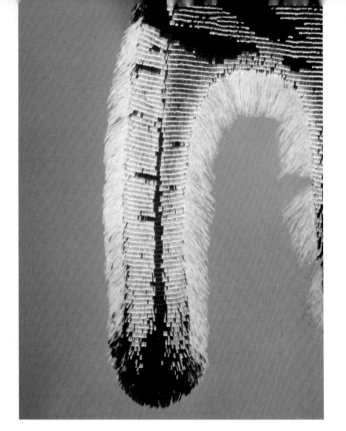

180. *far left:* Uraniidae: *Chrysiridia madagascariensis,* Madagascar. The underside of the hind wing.

181. *left:* Uraniidae: *Chrysiridia madagascariensis,* Madagascar. Close-up of a tail.

182. *below left:* Uraniidae: *Chrysiridia madagascariensis,* Madagascar. This day-flying African moth has been called the most beautiful insect in the world. The unique structure of its scales produces a brilliance that is unsurpassed, and the fringes of its triple tails, like the soft terminal feathers on the wings of owls, help to make flight silent.

183. *right:* Saturniidae: *Copiopteryx semiramis,* Venezuela. Not only its trailing tails but a fantastic pattern and coloring that create the illusion of a third dimension help to protect this moth.

184. *below:* Papilionidae: *Lamproptera meges,* Malaya. Few butterflies are more exotic than this beautiful insect, with its glassy fore-wing tips, bright turquoise band, and waving tails that give it a length of nearly 8 centimeters. It is usually found, as shown here, drinking moisture from sand.

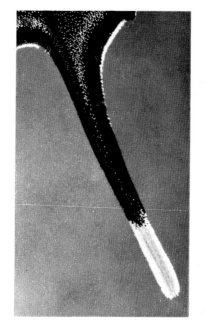

185. *opposite:* Papilionidae: *Papilio rutulus,* United States. This butterfly, called the Western tiger swallowtail, differs from the Eastern tiger *(Papilio glaucus)* in the markings on the edge of the underside of the fore wings. In the Western species this edge has a fine yellow line. In the Eastern tiger the same edge is decorated with fine yellow elongated crescents.

186. *above:* Papilionidae: *Graphium protesilaus,* Brazil. This spread specimen clearly shows the unusual length of the butterfly, due to the long, pointed fore wings and exceptionally long tails. These characteristics have a protective function, in that a bird predator may snap out a section of wing, missing the more vital area of the insect's body.

187. *above right:* Papilionidae: *Teinopalpus imperialis,* Sikkim. The male has only one tail on each hind wing. The female has three, which may give her extra protection if she is attacked during the time of egg laying.

188. *above far right:* Papilionidae: *Atroplaneura rhodifer,* Andaman Islands. The tails of this butterfly end in a conspicuous red "teardrop."

189. *right:* Papilionidae: *Papilio thaos,* Brazil. This lovely South American butterfly is so closely related to our North American *Papilio cresphontes* that they can be told apart only by the difference in size of one small yellow spot. This specimen is spread to accentuate the dramatic effect of the broad yellow band, which is both disruptive and startling.

hind wings. The green tails of the kaiserihind, an Oriental swallowtail (*Teinopalpus imperialis*), are tipped with gold, and the black tails of *Papilio rhodifer* end in red teardrops. *Chrysiridia madagascariensis*, in addition to its tails, has magnificent patches of red and gold iridescence on both the upper and lower sides of its hind wings. Many butterflies which have no tails have borders of metallic or scintillating colored scales. Perhaps it may be said that any sharply contrasting color, metallic glitter, or unusual shape on the hind-wing border protects a butterfly in flight by drawing the attention of birds away from its body. So it is that some of the most spectacular aspects of a butterfly are those which protect it best.

All of these scraps of knowledge, however marvelous they may be, are but fragments painstakingly gathered over hundreds of years. When pieced together, they hardly begin to solve the enigma of the most beautiful insect in the world. Butterflies see in each other movement and color which we do not see. Other animals see in butterflies things which the butterflies themselves cannot see. What we see in that fleeting moment of grace when a butterfly settles on a flower is the essence of all lovely things. If we, like the Chinese Buddhist, quietly contemplate a butterfly, what may we not see on its wings! A rainbow, a sky bright with stars, windows of colored glass, shimmering silks and jeweled robes, a summer meadow, or a temple sheathed in gold—the sources of inspiration and wonder which have sustained man's need for beauty through untold generations.

Had I the heaven's embroidered cloths
Enwrought with golden and silver light
The blue and the dim and the dark cloths
Of night and light and the half light,
I would lay the cloths under your feet. . . .
FRANCIS THOMPSON

There are remarkable similarities between the designs on the wings of butterflies and moths and those on ancient fabrics from many parts of the world, fabrics that originated in times when man was in much closer harmony with nature than he is today. Some wings have the gossamer delicacy of Oriental silks, others have a Victorian opulence. And even with today's uninhibited use of color and design butterfly wings can be found that are no less bold in concept and no less psychedelic in hue than the most contemporary fabrics.

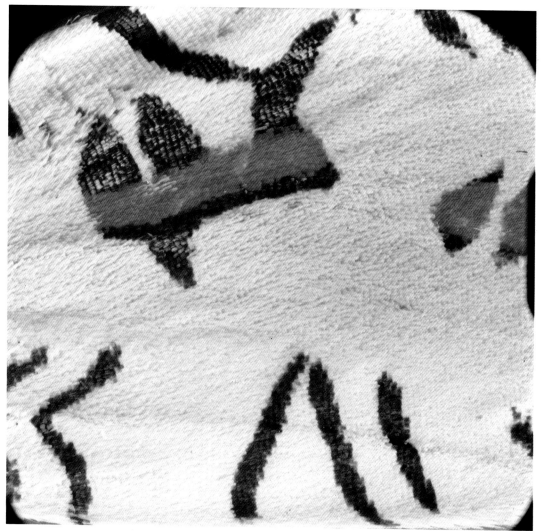

190. Noctuidae, Congo.

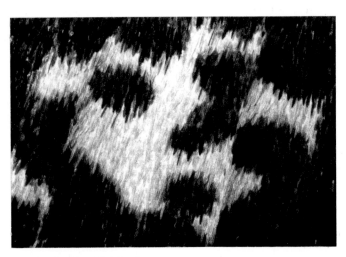

191. Sphingidae, Zululand.

192. Nymphalidae: *Charaxes tiridates,* Cameroun.

193. *below:* Acraeidae: *Acraea ranavalona,* Madagascar.

194. Nymphalidae: *Prepona amesia,* Peru.

195. Saturniidae, China.

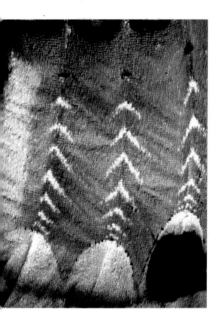

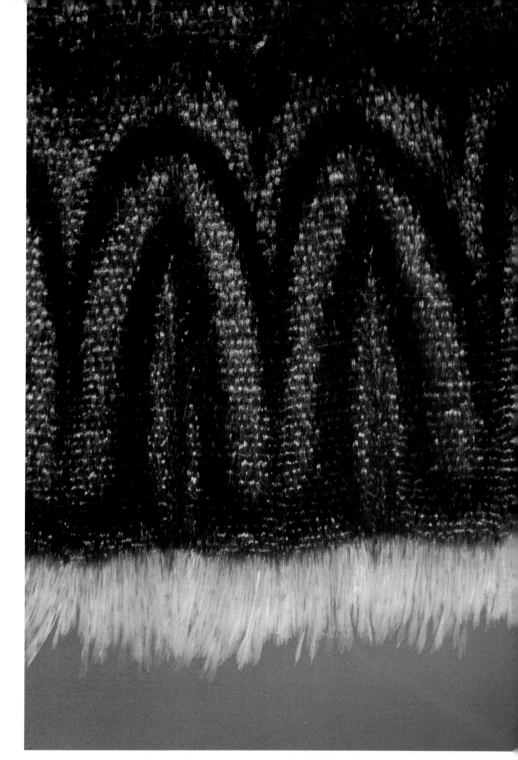

197. Noctuidae, Australia.

96. Pieridae: *Mylothris spica,* Cameroun.

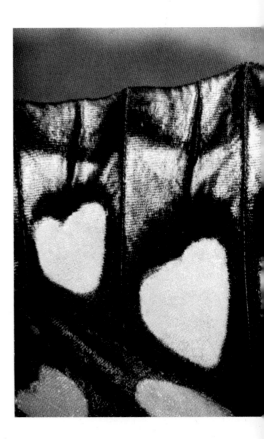

198. *left:* Lycaenidae: *Lachnocnema bibulus,* Malawi.

199. Papilionidae: *Papilio theorini,* Africa.

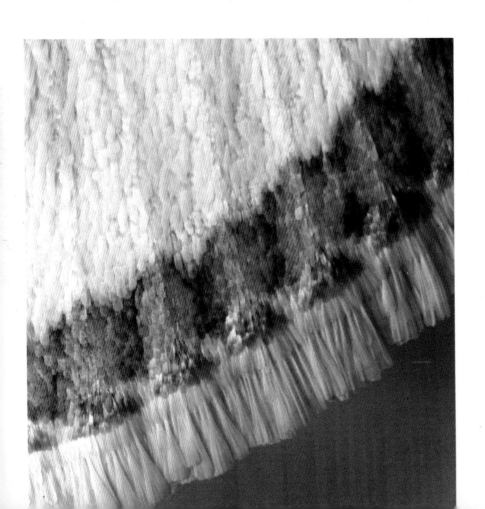

200. *left:* Xylorictidae, Australia.

201. Sphingidae, Australia.

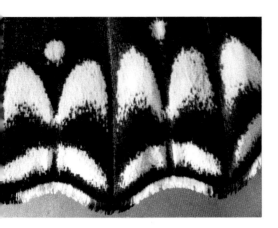

202. Nymphalidae: *Hypolimnas sp.,* Mindanao.

203. Nymphalidae: *Eriboea athamas,* India.

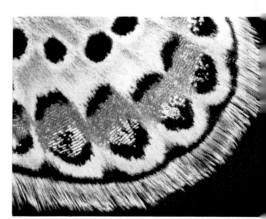

204. Lycaenidae: *Lycaeides melissa,* United States.

*Overleaf:*
205. Zygaenidae, China.

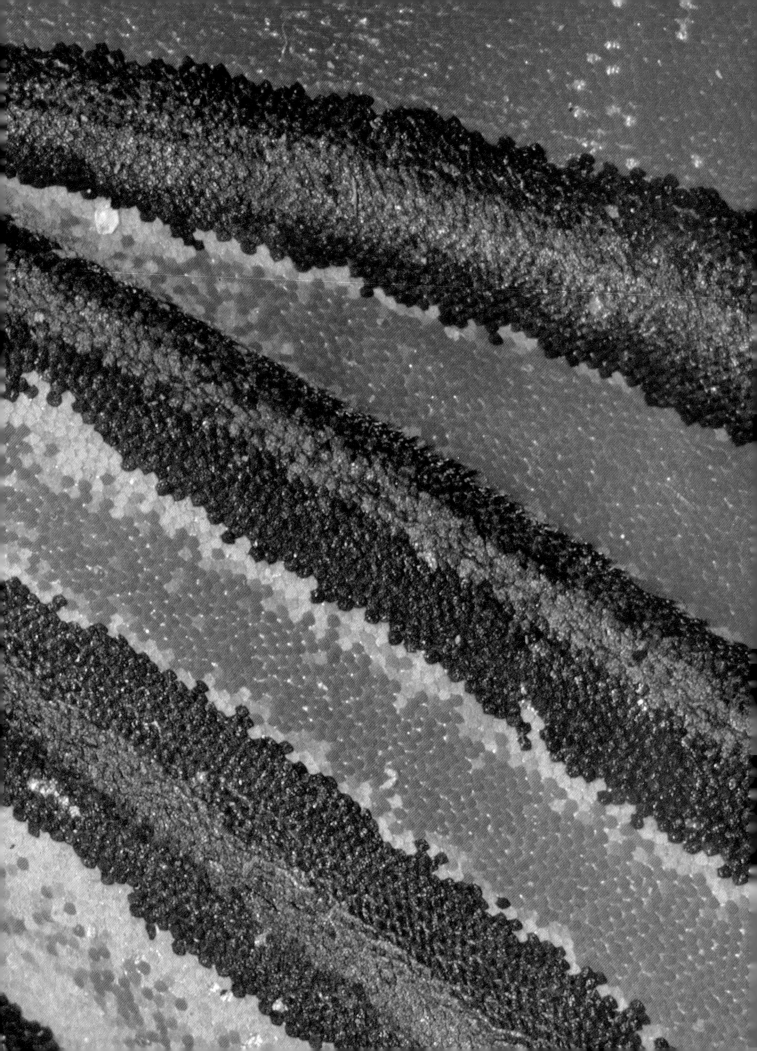

206. *below:* Pieridae: *Anteos menippe,* Brazil. Almost all sulphur butterflies snap their wings closed immediately upon alighting and do not open them again until the next time they fly. Hardly any have the habit of basking with open wings. This small sulphur is one that does. (Posed specimen.)

207. *opposite top:* Papilionidae: *Papilio rothschildi,* New Guinea.

208. *opposite middle:* Pieridae: *Phoebis rurina,* Costa Rica. Hairlike scales form this flowery pattern on the underside of the wing where it is attached to the butterfly's thorax.

209. *opposite bottom:* Papilionidae: *Archon apollinus,* Syria. Like the Parnassians, to which they are allied, these butterflies inhabit the mountains, flying at about 5000 feet. This is a rather small butterfly, about 2 inches across. This design is found on the lower border of the hind wings.

*verleaf:*

0. Nymphalidae: *Callicore sp.,* Peru. Several tterflies with this pattern on the underwings ve been called the 88 or 89 butterflies. They nnot be accurately identified without detailed udy. Some species are streaked with descent blue on the dorsal side, others with een or purple.

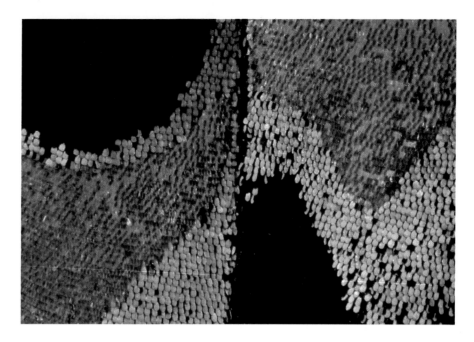

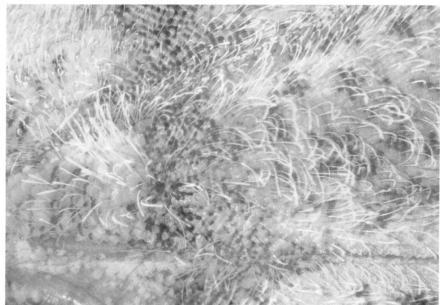

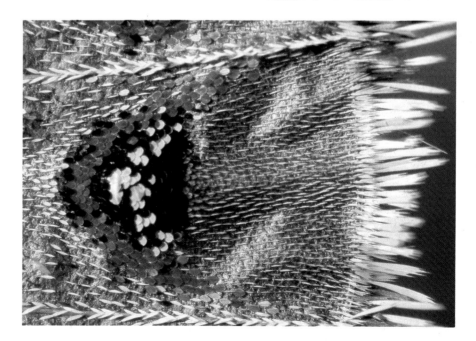

It has sometimes been asserted that the designs which occur in the wings of Lepidoptera follow certain limiting rules—that there are only a few basic wing patterns, and that all wings are variations of these. From a technical point of view, this may indeed be true. There are eyespots, bands, lunules, streaks, and so on, which can appear in a predictable number of combinations.

But from an artistic point of view, no such limitations exist. Each whole wing is a masterpiece composed of an endless number of details which, however small, are masterpieces also. The beauty of many such wings, or fragments of them, is not revealed to the naked eye, but through the lenses of certain cameras or through a microscope a dazzling panorama comes to life which can hardly be enhanced by information of a technical sort. It stands as eloquent proof of an earlier statement, which was that any contribution made by a butterfly must remain secondary to its aesthetic worth.

The plates that follow all show fragments of the wings of butterflies and moths. Some are details the size of a thumbnail. Others cover areas no larger than a poppy seed. In them is the essence of all beautiful things. In them is made manifest the awesome secret of a magnificence too small—or perhaps too great—for human eyes to see.

"The wonder of the world, the beauty and the power, the shapes of things, their colors, lights, and shades; these I saw. Look ye also while life lasts" (from "Wapiti Wilderness" by Margaret and Olaus Murie).

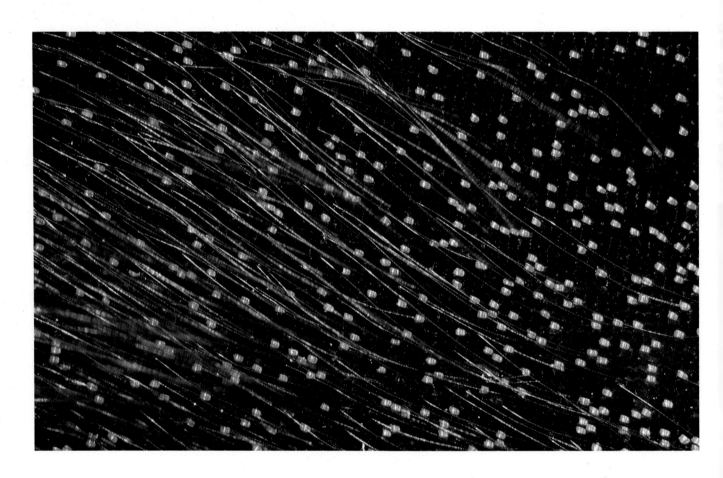

211. Papilionidae: *Ornithoptera priamus urvilleanus,* Solomon Islands.

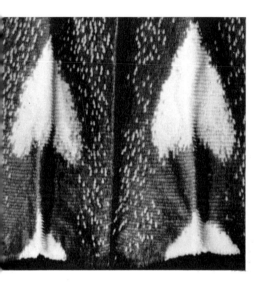

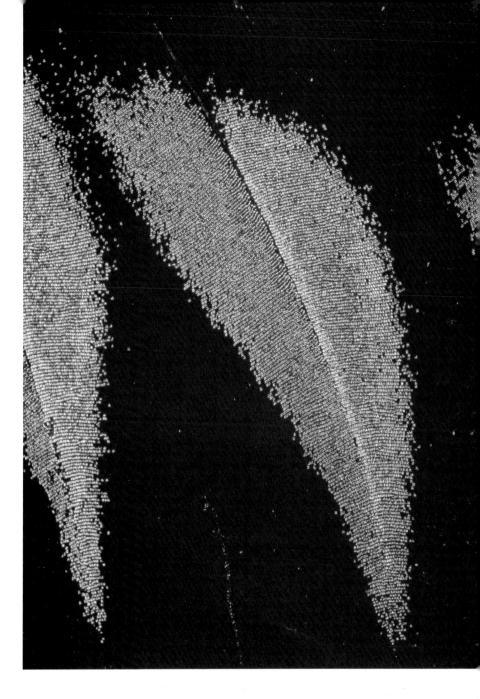

212. *above:* Papilionidae: *Papilio dravidarum*, India.

213. *right:* Papilionidae: *Trogonoptera brookiana,* Borneo. A leafy fore-wing border gives grace as well as effective camouflage to this birdwing butterfly of the tropical jungle. (For a full view of this butterfly, see plate 18.)

214. *below:* Papilionidae: *Ornithoptera priamus croesus,* Philippines.

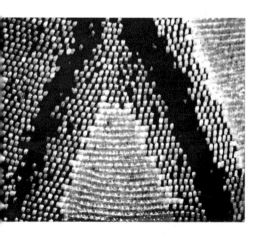

215. *right:* Riodinidae: *Lymnas pixe,* Mexico.

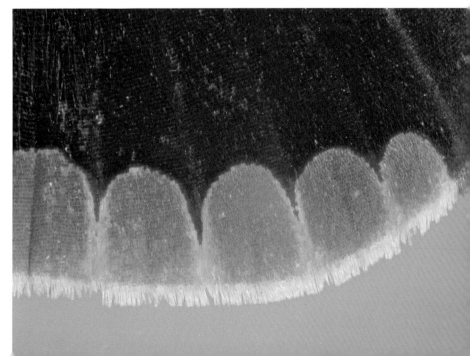

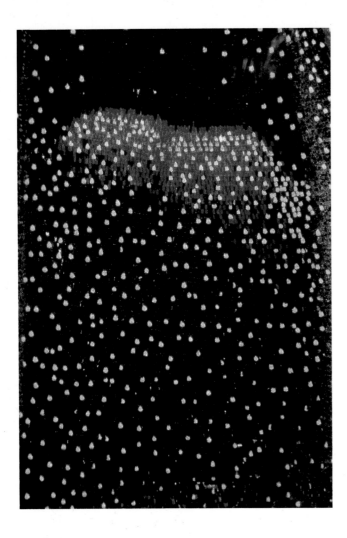

216. *above:* Papilionidae: *Papilio krishna,* Sikkim. The "star-fall" effect in this detail comes from a small section of the hind wing, magnified fifteen to twenty times. The actual area covered by these scales is about two square millimeters. The number of scales needed to cover all four wings is about 250,000.

217. *right:* Morphidae: *Morpho sp.,* Peru. The microscope gives up some of the secrets of the Morpho's blue fire.

 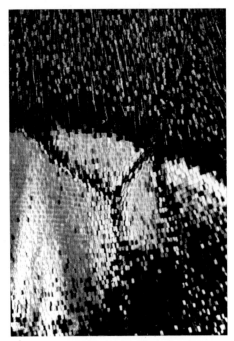

218. *far left:* Papilionidae: *Papilio troilus,* United States.

219. *left:* Papilionidae: *Teinopalpus imperialis,* China.

220. *below:* Castniidae, French Guiana.

221. *opposite:* Papilionidae: *Papilio krishna,* Sikkim. A detail of the wing, showing pigmented scales (red) and structurally colored scales reflecting lavender, green, and gold light.

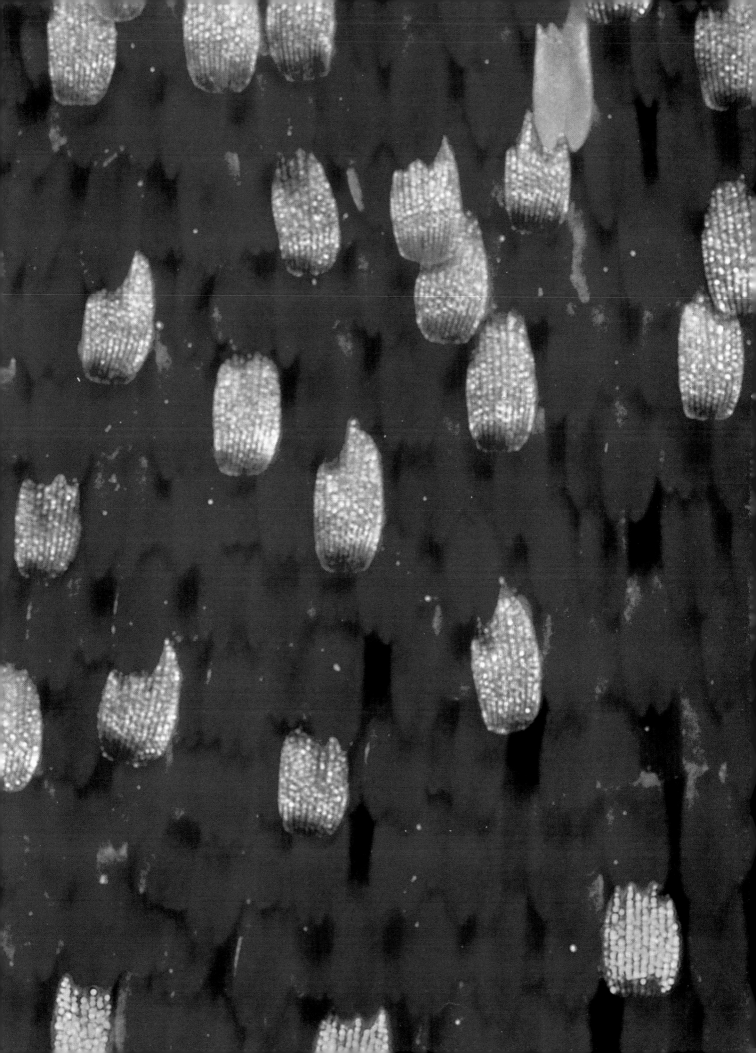

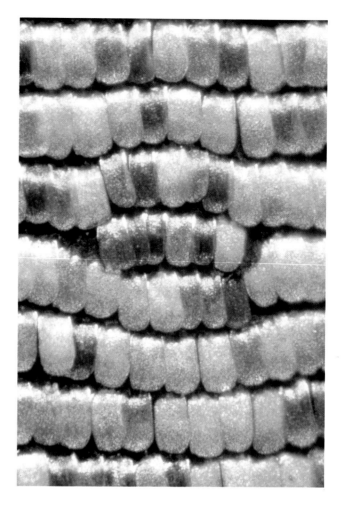

222. *opposite:* Castniidae, Guiana. In this design, occurring on the underside of the wing of a small moth, there is an inspirational quality akin to that which is sometimes found in abstract painting.

223. *above:* Papilionidae: *Ornithoptera priamus poseidon,* New Guinea. On this part of the wing, scales form a tight sheath shifting in color from pearl to gold.

224. *below:* Papilionidae: *Papilio paris splendorifer,* Borneo. A butterfly's wings are always in harmony. This softly beautiful pattern of mahogany and pale green transversed by long, threadlike scales occurs on the underside of the butterfly's hind wing.

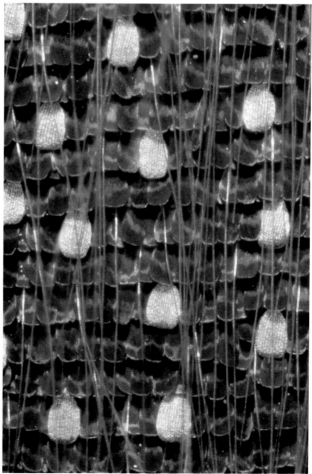

159

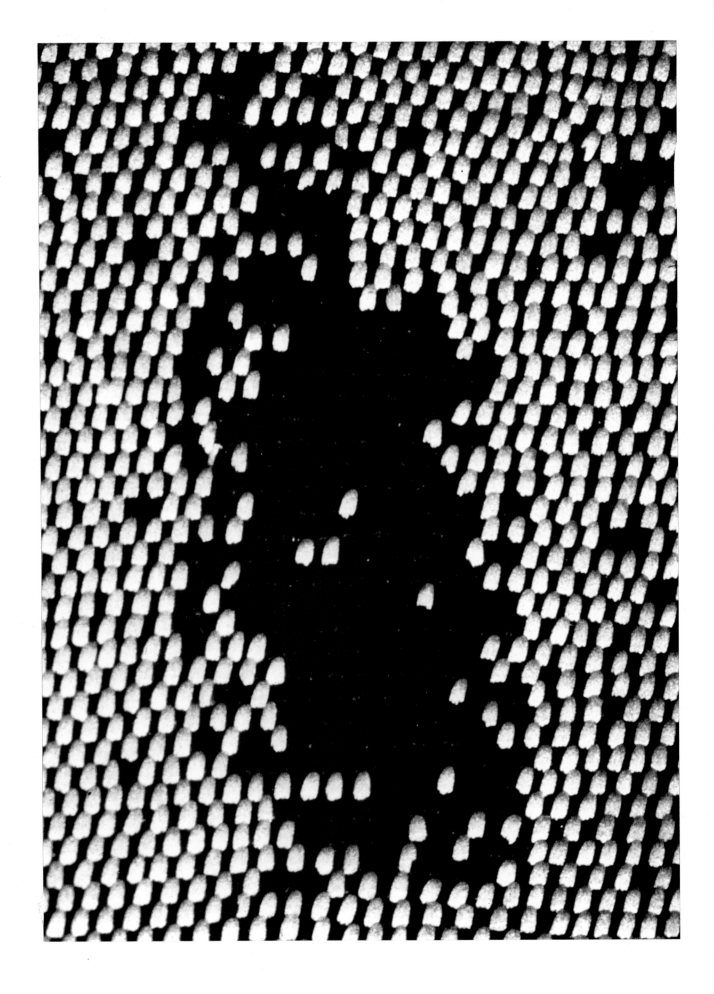

225. *opposite:* Papilionidae: *Ornithoptera priamus croesus,* Philippines.

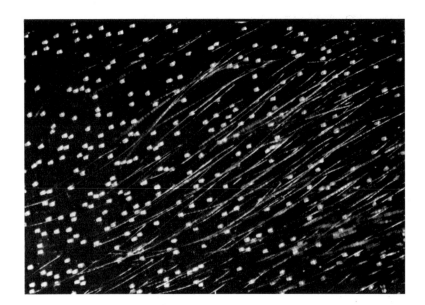

226. Papilionidae: *Ornithoptera priamus urvilleanus,* Solomon Islands.

227. *below:* Papilionidae: *Teinopalpus imperialis,* Sikkim.

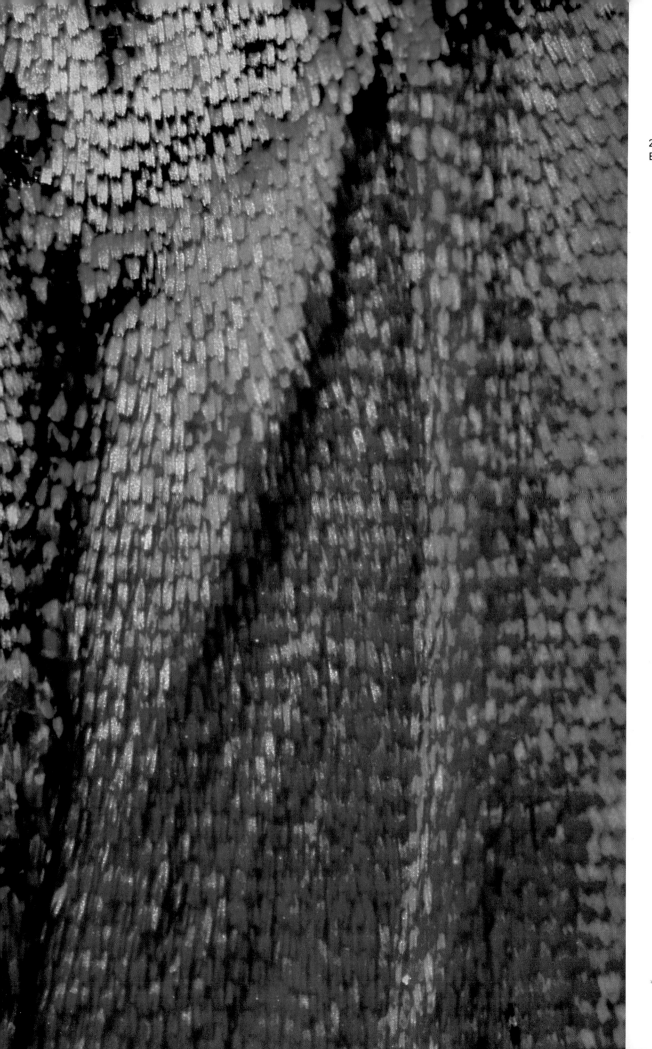

228. Geometridae,
Ecuador.

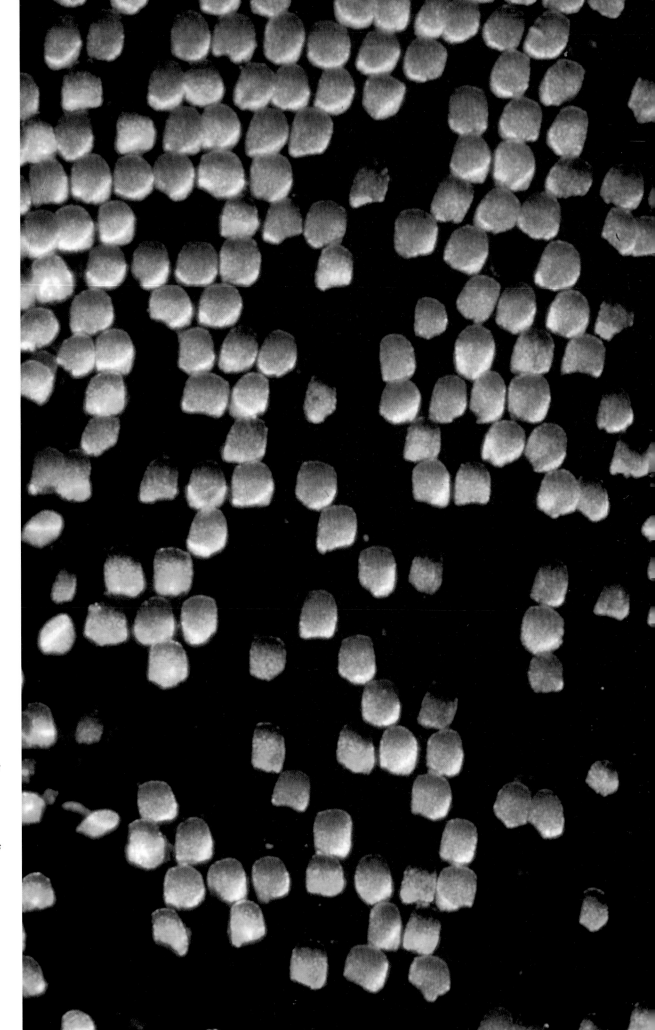

29. Papilionidae:
*Ornithoptera priamus
euphorion,* Austfalia.

*Overleaf:*
30. Papilionidae:
*Ornithoptera priamus
croesus,* Philippines.

231. *above:* Papilionidae: *Papilio paris,* New Guinea. Th
is another of the green-spangled swallowtails. It is nea
all black with a thin overlay of shining green. When ligh
glances across the wings of these butterflies as they fly
from flower to flower, it gives them a jewel-like sparkle.
On the margin of each hind wing there is a small deep-
orange and lavender ring, both above and beneath. The
detail of the same butterfly (plate 233) is a microscopic
section of the orange and lavender spot on one of the
hind wings. The deep-orange scales are bordered with
iridescent lavender scales, a few of which are scattered
among the pigmented scales.

232. *left:* Pericopidae, South America.

233. *opposite:* Papilionidae: *Papilio paris,* Sikkim.

*Overleaf:*
234. Lycaenidae: *Eumaeus minyas,* Costa Rica. This
butterfly is a close relation of the very scarce *Eumaeus
atala,* a native of Florida that some entomologists think
may be extinct.

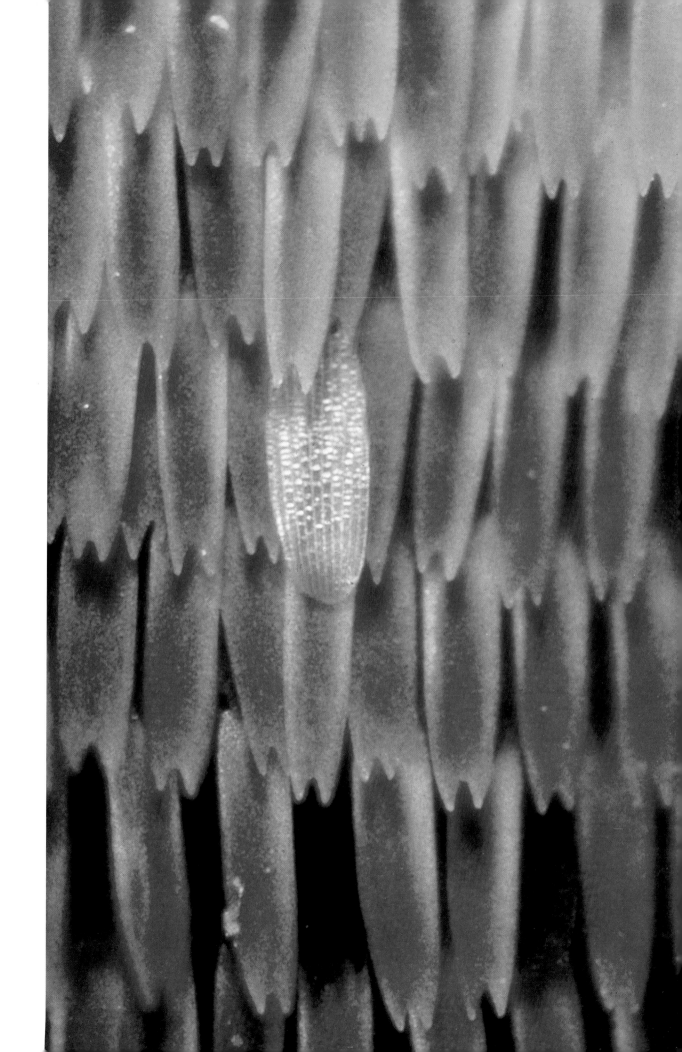

*The Lepidopterist*

The lepidopterist with happy cries
Devotes his days to hunting butterflies.
The leopard, through some feline mental twist,
Would rather hunt a lepidopterist.
That's why I never adopted lepidoptery;
I do not wish to live in jeopardoptery.

OGDEN NASH

Seldom, if ever, is a butterfly given any humorous connotations, unless it falls into the consciousness of a very whimsical poet—or of a very perceptive photographer.

235. Nymphalidae: *Cethosia biblis.* Sikkim.

# BIBLIOGRAPHY

Anton, Ferdinand, and Dockstader, Frederick. *Pre-Columbian Art and Later Indian Tribal Arts.* New York: Harry N. Abrams, 1968.

Aubert, Jacques. *Papillons d'Europe.* Neuchatel, Switzerland: Editions Delachaux & Niestle, 1961.

Barcant, Malcolm. *Butterflies of Trinidad and Tobago.* London: Collins, 1970.

Bastin, Harold. *Insects.* New York: Frederick Stokes, 1913.

Blunt, Wilfred. *The Compleat Naturalist, A Life of Linnaeus.* New York: Viking Press, 1971.

Brower, Lincoln P. "Ecological Chemistry," *Scientific American,* vol. 220, no. 2 (Feb. 1969).

Brower, Lincoln Pierson; Brower, Jane Van Zandt; and Cranston, Florence Pitkin. "Courtship Behavior of the Queen Butterfly, *Danaus gilippus berenice* (Cramer). *Zoologica* (New York Zoological Society), vol. 50, issue 1 (1965).

Burns, Alexander. *Australian Butterflies.* Sydney: A. H. and A. W. Reed, 1969.

Burns, John M. "Preferential Mating and Mimicry. Disruptive Selection and Sex-Limited Dimorphism in *P. glaucus,*" *Science,* vol. 153, no. 3735 (July 29, 1966).

Clarke, C. A. "The Prevention of 'Rhesus' Babies," *Scientific American,* vol. 219, no. 22 (Nov. 1968).

Clench, Harry K. "Behavioral Thermoregulation in Butterflies," *Ecology,* vol. 47, no. 6.

Comstock, J. H. *An Introduction to Entomology* (9th ed., rev.). Ithaca, N. Y.: Cornell University, 1964.

Covarrubias, Miguel. *Indian Art of Mexico and Central America.* New York: Alfred A. Knopf, 1957.

Cumont, F. Valerie. *Recherches sur le symbolisme funéraire des Romains.* Paris: P. Genther, 1942.

de Roover, Florence Edler. "Lucchese Silks," *CIBA Review* (Basel), June 1950.

Duffy, S. S. "Cardiac Glycosides and Distastefulness," *Science,* vol. 169, no. 3940 (July 1970).

Eltringham, E. *African Mimetic Butterflies.* London: Clarendon Press, 1910.

Evans, Howard Ensign. *Life on a Little-known Planet.* New York: E. P. Dutton, 1968.

Ford, E. B. *Butterflies.* London: Collins, 1962.

Franco, José Luis C. *Representaciones de la Mariposa en Mesoamerica.*

Handschin, E. "Silk Moths," *CIBA Review* (Basel), Nov. 1946.

Holland, W. J. *The Butterfly Book.* New York: Doubleday Page, 1914.

——. *The Moth Book.* New York: Doubleday Page, 1914.

Jougla de Morenas, Henri. *Grand Armorial de France,* 7 vols. Paris: Les Editions Héraldiques, 1934–52.

Kevan, P. G., and Shorthouse, J. D. "Behavioral Thermoregulation by High Arctic Butterflies." Entomological Research Institute, Canada Department of Agriculture and Defense Research Board of Canada, Ottawa. *Studies on Arctic Insects,* 23, no. 4 (Dec. 1970).

King, Charles William. *Antique Gems and Rings.* London: Bell and Daldy, 1872.

237. Nymphalidae: *Charaxes tiridates*, Cameroun.

238. Saturniidae, Malawi.

Klots, A. B. *A Field Guide to the Butterflies*. Boston: Houghton Mifflin, 1951.

———. *The World of Butterflies and Moths*. New York: McGraw-Hill, n. d.

Larousse World Mythology. *Central America: Gods of Sacrifice*. New York: Putnam, 1965.

Leech, John Henry. *Butterflies from China, Japan and Korea*. London: R. H. Porter, 1892–94.

Geliot, Louvan. *La vraye et parfait science des armoires*. Paris: E. Rouveyre, 1895 (originally published 1560).

MacCulloch, John A., ed. *Mythology of All Races*. Volume II: *Latin America*. Lincoln: University of Nebraska, 1932.

McManus, T. F. *A Century of Glass Manufacture, 1818–1918*. Toledo, Ohio: Toledo Glass Co., 1918.

*Manuel de l'armateur de reliures armoriées françaises*. Paris: Ch. Bosse, libraire, 1938.

Michener, James A. *Japanese Prints from the Early Masters to the Modern*. Rutland, Vt.: Charles E. Tuttle, 1959.

Morrell, R. *Common Malayan Butterflies*. London: Longmans Green, 1960.

Packard, A. S. *Textbook of Entomology*. New York: Macmillan, 1898.

Parsons, Elsie Crew. *Mitla—Town of the Souls*. Evanston, Ill.: University of Chicago Press, 1936.

Pettit, G. R.; Houghton, L. E.; Rogers, N. H.; Coomes, R. M.; Berger, D. F.; Reucroft, P. R.; and Day, J. F., Arizona State University. Hartwell, J. L., and Wood, H. B., Jr., National Cancer Institute, Bethesda, Md. "Butterfly Wing Antineoplastic Agents." Part 27 of a series of unpublished papers. Presented before the American Chemical Society, Washington, D. C., 1971.

Priest, Alan. "Insects: The Philosopher and the Butterfly," *The Metropolitan Museum of Art Bulletin* (New York), Feb. 1952.

Reichstein, T.; von Euw, J.; Parsons, J. A.; and Rothschild, Miriam. "Heart Poisons in the Monarch Butterfly," *Science*, vol. 161, no. 3844 (Aug. 30, 1968)

172

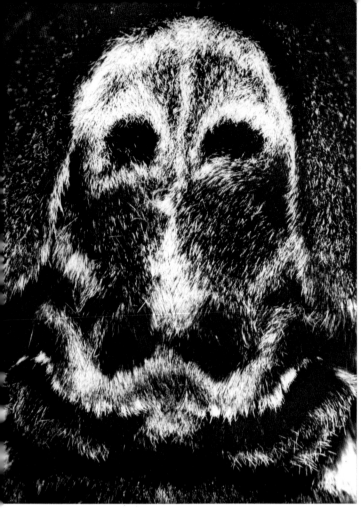

239. Sphingidae: *Acherontia sp.,* India. Strange markings on the thorax have earned for members of this genus the name of death-head moths.

240. Nymphalidae: *Polygrapha cyanea,* Peru.

Revi, A. C. *Nineteenth-Century Cut Glass—Its Genesis and Development.* New York: Nelson, 1959.

Richter, Gisela. *Catalogue of Engraved Gems of the Classical Style.* New York: The Metropolitan Museum of Art, 1920.

Rothschild, Miriam. "Mimicry," *Natural History,* vol. LXXVI, no. 2 (Feb. 1967).

Soustelle, Jacques. *The Arts of Ancient Mexico.* New York: Viking Press, 1967.

Spretti, Vittorio. *Enciclopedia Storico Nobilaire Italiana.* Milan: 1928.

Stratton, Arthur. *The Great Red Island.* New York: Scribner, 1964.

Urquhart, Fred A. *The Monarch Butterfly.* University of Toronto Press, 1960.

Urquhart, F. A. "Monarch Butterfly Migration Studies," *Proceedings Ent. Soc. Ontario (1964),* 1965.

———. "A Study of the Migrations of the Gulf Coast Population of the Monarch Butterfly (*Danaus plexippus L.*) in North America," *Ann. Zool. Fenn. 3,* 1966.

Valliant, George C. Revised by Suzannah B. Valliant. *Aztecs of Mexico.* New York: Doubleday & Co., Inc., 1962.

Vermeule, Cornelius C., III. *The Dal Pozzo-Albani Drawings of Classical Antiquities in the Royal Library of Windsor Castle.* Philadelphia: American Philosophical Society, 1966.

Warner, Ralph. *Dutch and Flemish Flowers and Fruit Painters.* London: Mills & Boon, 1928.

Werner, E. T. C. *Myths and Legends of China.* New York: Brentano.

Williams, Carrol M. "The Juvenile Hormone," *Scientific American,* Feb. 1958.

Williams, C. B. "Butterfly Travellers," *National Geographic,* vol. LXXI, no. 5 (May 1937).

Williams, John G. *Field Guide to the Butterflies of Africa.* Boston: Houghton Mifflin, 1971.

Yoshaiki, Obara. "Studies on the Mating Behavior of the White Cabbage Butterfly, *Pieris rapae crucivora* (*Bois.*), no. III, *Z. Vergl. Physiologie 66,* 99–116, 1970.

# INDEX OF ILLUSTRATED BUTTERFLIES

242. Sphingidae: *Hemeroplanes unuus,* Mexico. This is the only American genus of sphinx moths having a silvery spot on the fore wing. There is on one species in the United States; the others inhab tropical America.

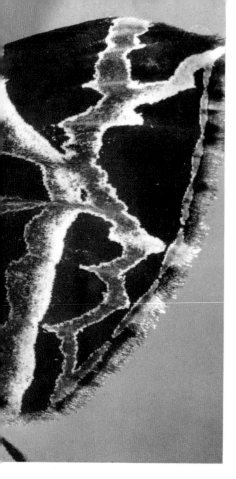

243. Geometridae, Ecuador.

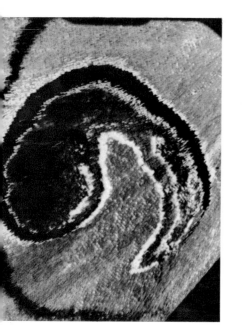

244. Noctuidae, Malawi.

# INDEX OF ILLUSTRATED MOTH FAMILIES

*The numbers refer to plate numbers;*
*colorplates are indicated by an asterisk.* \*

245. Nymphalidae:
*Prepona amesia,*
Peru.

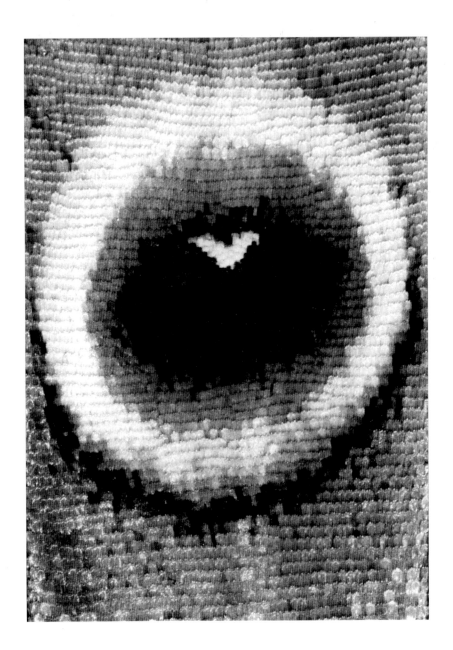

# PHOTOGRAPH CREDITS

All the photographs of butterflies and moths used for this book were provided by Kjell B. Sandved with the exception of the following:

George W. Brewer: 50, 53, 59; Jo Brewer: 49, 51, 54, 61, 70, 73–77; Dr. Donald R. Davis: 117, 132, 134–37